BIRTH

BEGINS

at

40

CHALLENGING THE MYTHS
ABOUT LATER MOTHERHOOD

CORINNE SWEET

Acorn Independent Press

To Bobbie and Marika who made all the difference in the world

Contents

Acknowledgments vii

Introduction 1

1   My Own Story 5

2   Myth 1: Past it at Forty
    Reality today: Forty is the new thirty 29

3   Myth 2: Granny at the School Gate
    Reality today: Late parents make great parents 53

4   Myth 3: Older Bodies Can't Take the Strain
    Reality today: Women have never been fitter 85

5   Myth 4: Disabled Women Over Forty Can't Have Children
    *Reality today: Disabled mothers over
    forty are perfectly able* 103

6   Myth 5: Only is Lonely
    Reality today: Lone parents over forty are fine 125

7   Myth 6: No Baby at Over Forty, No Children in Your Life
    *Reality today: You can have children in your
    life at over forty without giving birth* 141

8   Myth 7: It's Not Fair on Babies to Have Them at Over Forty
    Reality today: Better late than never 173

Further Reading 185

Acknowledgments

Thanks to Leila Green of Acorn Publications; Jane Graham Maw of Graham Maw Christie and to Clara Potter-Sweet for all her wonderful help. Also thanks to Johnny McKeown for his support and encouragement. Thanks too, to Ben Walker and Rosa Garland.

Heartfelt thanks to Carole Blake, my agent at Blake Friedmann, and to Judith Longman, my editor at Hodder, who both expertly encouraged and 'midwifed' this book into life. Thanks too, to Susi Rogol, ex-Editor of *Home & Life* magazine, Sharon Parsons, ex-Editor of *Top Sante Health & Beauty,* and Saska Graville, ex-Editor of *New Woman* (Australia) for advertising for interviewees and for running my articles on late motherhood. Also thanks to Sophie Jopson, producer at Liberty Radio for making a special programme on older mums.

Thanks and gratitude to Julia Berryman of the Parenthood Research Group at the University of Leicester for her professional input and excellent ongoing research on the benefits of late motherhood. Eternal thanks to Mr Anthony Silverstone and Ms Melanie Davies, Consultant Obstetricians at University College Hospital, and to all their wonderful staff for helping me have my own child when I was forty-three and from whom I learned so much. Thanks to Professor Lesley Regan of Obstetrics and Gynaecology and the Recurrent Miscarriage Unit at St Mary's Hospital, Paddington, for her expert care, ongoing research and advice. Thanks to my National Childbirth Trust teacher, Diana Parkinson, and my group (especially Suzanne Stapleton and Pet Chaplin) for all the support and encouragement I was given in becoming a late mother myself. A big thank you, too, to Emily Papaloizou and all the fantastic staff (especially Lynne, Alison, Marlene, Christina and Helen) at Alexandra Day Nursery, and to Hayley Baker, Jacki Thompson and

Gaby Bikhazi, without whose fabulous childcare help this book would never have been written.

Much love and thanks to Corinne Haynes (especially for reading the manuscript of this book) and Albert Haynes, Regina and Peter McLennan, Chris Blackie, Sue Pratt, Romilly Gregory, Irene Inskip, Penny Deans, Rebecca Jay, Alexandra Campbell, Susan Quilliam, Virginia Ironside, Christine Archer, Lizzie Smith, Armorer Wason and Sally Potter for their insight, friendship, support and practical help. Thanks and love, as always, to Marika Denton and Margaret Evans. Finally, the biggest, warmest, snuggliest hugs to Rufus, Clara and Splat for supporting, encouraging and putting up with me throughout the throes of giving birth to this book.

A Word on Interviewees

Many thanks to the women and men who opened their hearts to me about the issue of having children late in life. All the interviews in this book are genuine. Some names and locations have been changed to protect their identities due to personal considerations, such as the impact of sensitive information on family, friends, ex-partners/husbands and work colleagues.

Introduction

Kate Hudson, America Ferrera, Salma Hayek, Madonna, Cherie Blair, Iman, Koo Stark, Jerry Hall, Emma Thompson — what have all these women got in common? *They've all had babies over the age of forty.* Celebrities have led the way in having babies later in life, due to having the money, time, staff and private medical care available to support them, and thus thousands of 'ordinary' women are being inspired to do so too. In fact, late mothers are hot news: on 21 June 2001, the day this book was first published, Lynne Bezant became the oldest woman to give birth to twins in Britain, at the age of fifty-six. A day hardly passes without at least one story in the newspapers announcing yet another 'miracle' birth to a woman in her forties, fifties, or even sixties or seventies.

According to the Office for National Statistics, growing numbers of women are choosing to have their babies later in life. At the start of the twenty-first century, the average age for first-time births is nudging thirty, whereas a century ago it was twenty-one. The average age for a first time birth is now 31 years old. 40 per cent of babies are born to women aged between thirty and thirty-nine, with two per cent being born to women forty plus. The trend looks set to continue as women decide to put off having babies until their careers are established and/or the right man comes along. The possibility of women freezing their eggs early in life may mean women will choose to bypass their twenties and thirties altogether and have their children at forty plus. Advances in technology, improvements in women's health and fitness, as well as greater affluence and better education, mean that women are in a better position than ever before to 'have it all'. A career woman today does not necessarily have to sacrifice the whole of her life to her job - she can probably have a baby, too, when she is ready. 'Being ready' denotes being emotionally equipped enough to have a child

1

and/or having the right relationship in place. Physical illness and disability, which would have been perceived as a barrier to motherhood thirty years ago, can be treatable today. And the exponential growth of the infertility industry is giving hope to thousands of women who had virtually given up on motherhood.

When I got pregnant myself for the first time at forty-two in 1996, I rushed to the bookshops to find something to read about what I might experience. There was absolutely nothing for me: all the books told me I had been 'old' at thirty-five, so forty-two was off the scale. Positively geriatric, I was told. Even prestigious pregnancy writers, such as Sheila Kitzinger and Miriam Stoppard, hardly mentioned forty-plus mothers at all.

I wanted to know what I might be up against, what I might have to face, and I wanted to hear from other women. How long did it take them to get pregnant? Did they have fertility treatment or could they get pregnant naturally? Did they have all the age-related screening tests or did they risk foetal abnormality? Had they had previous miscarriages? Were they worried about disability - their own and the baby's? Were they able to have natural births or did they have to have a Caesarian? How had their families reacted? What happened about work? What sort of childcare would they opt for? Were they worried about being older? Were they in a relationship and how did late motherhood affect it? And what did they do if the pregnancy failed and they couldn't have children? How did they have children in their life?

Finding nothing to guide me, I have myself written the book I wanted to read. The absence of books on mothers over forty reflects our need to deny that women are having babies at forty plus - almost as if we don't want to encourage it. It's clear that, as a good forty-year-old woman friend put it to me, there is a 'forest of myths' surrounding late motherhood. Ageism and sexism (yes, they unfortunately do still exist) mean that we are generally much harder on women who have babies late in life than we are on men.

We hardly raise an eyebrow to David Jason having a baby at sixty-one or Tony Blair at forty-six; we smile at the prospect of *Star Trek's* Scotty having a child at eighty-three, or the late David Bowie at fifty-three; we think it's fine that Michael Douglas had a new baby at fifty-five, or Phil Collins at forty-nine. But if a woman has a baby over forty, even fifty, she is often dismissed as irresponsible, selfish or unfit. Stereotypes abound about what women should or should not be doing over the age of forty. And yet, like the celebrity men mentioned above, many women only finally find happiness with the right person later in life, after many failed attempts at marriage and cohabitation. A baby can still be an emotional seal on a good love relationship, regardless of a couple's age. Of course, not everyone wants babies or can have babies, but those who do should be encouraged, not disparaged, if they are forty plus.

In fact, the reality today is that forty is the new thirty: forty, fifty and even sixty ain't what they used to be. Women are fitter, healthier, more active, sexually demanding, more engaged with life at all levels, than ever before. And the truth is that older mothers can be absolutely brilliant mothers. They may not be stick-thin, unwrinkled and pure, but they have wisdom, life experience and patience on their side. When the fact that Lynne Bezant was expecting twins was announced in the *Mirror* in January 2001, Sally Weale of the *Guardian* Women's page surprisingly ran a reactionary article which tut-tutted about Bezant's age, suggesting that late pregnancy offends the rights of the unborn child. It took a man, George Monbiot, writing in the same paper to put things in perspective: 'What about the rights of children whose parents are too immature to respond to their needs? Is there any mother or father who would not have brought up their children differently, with the benefit of hindsight? Surely children whose parents have gone to enormous trouble to conceive are more likely to be loved than the accidents of a carefree fecundity?'

Indeed, research undertaken by Julia Berryman, ex-Senior Lecturer and head of the Parenthood Research Group at

Leicester University, supports the notion that late mothers are good mothers. Her work positively scotches the myths that older mums are out of touch, boring, emotionally damaging and physically incapable. Yes, they get tired - but so do most parents. More importantly, her research shows that children of older mothers achieve higher reading scores at an earlier age and have good social skills. The most significant factor is that the children are very much wanted and are deeply loved. A child who is wanted, loved and nurtured well by parents - regardless of their age - is surely something we should applaud in our culture, where so many children are discarded, neglected, abused, and even killed in extreme cases (as in the horrific deaths of eight-year-old Victoria Climbié in 2000, one-year-old Peter Connelly in 2007, and four-year-old Daniel Pelka in 2012 - stories of unbridled cruelty and torture which all shocked the nation).

It's never been a better time to push back the boundaries, not only with regard to our views of age and ageing, but also with regard to what actually constitutes being a good parent. We used to say 'life begins at forty' to counteract the feeling of dread that forty was the beginning of the end. Today, we need to say 'birth begins at forty' to reflect the amazing opportunities, choices and experiences open to many women facing mid-life today.

This book begins with my own story of having my one and only child at forty-three, and then moves on to examine the 'forest of myths' surrounding late motherhood. It presents a positive and inspiring alternative perspective, based on real-life interviews, which more accurately reflects the reality of late motherhood today.

1

My Own Story

Life begins at forty, or so the old saying goes. On my fortieth birthday I was single and alone, having recently ended a ten-year, childless marriage. I spent my actual birthday on an Arvon Foundation writer's course, drinking to my own health and future with a room full of fellow scribbling wannabes. That balmy summer night in Hebden Bridge I gave up on ever having a child. I gazed at the moon and stars thinking, 'If this is as good as it gets, then it'll be fine.' Yet, amazingly, barely three years later, I became a mum for the first time. For me, not only life but also birth began at forty.

It was a strange outcome for a life which I had led, up until my daughter's birth on 27 December 1996, as a person who would never, ever have children. I first made a decision not to have children when I was five. I distinctly remember thinking I never wanted to be a parent and that I would live happily without children as an adult. To some extent this was to do with being an only child. I used to sit on the window ledge at my primary school and watch the other children running around, feeling like a little grown-up. I'm sure I was fairly isolated and shy (with a patch over my glasses to strengthen a squint), but I can trace my proclivity for standing back, observing and analysing things (a deeply embedded writer's stance), to this point. I didn't particularly like other children - I found them frightening (I got punched in the stomach every day by a bullying little girl) - and I was not a child who played with dolls (I tore their clothes off and dropped them). I was much more interested in drawing, making up stories and talking to myself - something which remains true to this day. I experienced a lot of illness as a child, particularly asthma, bronchitis and pneumonia, so

I got used to spending hours alone in bed reading, doing puzzles and amusing myself. Consequently, I missed a lot of school (and loads of parties). I always wanted brothers and sisters, but it was not to be. Instead, I made them up.

At seventeen, I was run over by a ten-ton lorry while cycling to my Saturday job in the local library, and I nearly died. When I finally began to recover, I was told by a grumpy gynaecologist that I probably would never be able to have children. My pelvis and spine had been broken in five places, I had a broken right arm and several cracked ribs, plus many internal injuries. I spent a year in hospital and rehabilitation and on leaving, I was left with a feeling that it would definitely be life-threatening to procreate. This was coupled with the fact that I had a rare Rhesus-negative blood group, something which had caused problems for my own mother when she had me in the 1950s (she was Rh Neg, too). We'd both nearly died during my own protracted, difficult birth (my twin had been miscarried a month before). I didn't realise an antigen had been found which could be simply administered by injection to quash the effects of Rhesus-negative poisoning (the blood from the mother can cross to the foetus and vice versa, literally poisoning each other). I was also asthmatic and, I suppose, the overwhelming feeling I was left with about having babies was that it was far too dangerous a thing to do. I was determined to be a writer and I thought that having children would not fit in with such an esoteric pursuit. Having babies was something other people would do, not me.

I actually asked my GP to sterilise me when I was at university. I had fallen deeply in love with a German and, one night as we sat in the bar, I did actually have a flicker of 'I want this man's child'. He was aghast when I mentioned it and, at the time, it was impossible due to my recent accident injuries and our situation as impoverished students from different countries. I don't think either of us really took it that seriously, and then the moment was past. I was twenty-one, and so convinced that I would never want children that I asked the doctor if I could have the irreversible sterilization.

I remember the doctor looking down at his prescription pad for what seemed like ages, and then back at me, before saying he wouldn't do it. 'It's a serious decision to make at your age,' he had said sagely, 'go away and think about it. Anyway, you might change your mind in time.' I was very disappointed and angry because I felt he was being unfair and patronising. I knew what I wanted: I didn't want children. And I certainly didn't want to take a risk. I hated taking the Pill, which had nasty side effects back then.

However, the busyness of student life took over and I didn't pursue sterilisation. I threw myself into campaigning for legal abortion and women's rights: I suppose I channelled my fear of unwanted pregnancy thus. During my early twenties I was on the Pill, albeit reluctantly, and once I came off it, due to having twenty gallstones when I was twenty-five, I was scrupulous about not taking risks throughout my thirties.

Looking back, I think I was terrified of being pregnant and dying as a consequence. I also was convinced I would be a thoroughly inadequate mother due to my difficult childhood. I began training as a counsellor in 1979 and later joined a group of women counsellors who all felt ambivalent about having their own children. We called ourselves 'The Babies Group', and we met regularly over an eight-year period. Each of us had our own particular reasons for feeling divided on the subject of motherhood. For most of us, there were deep-seated feelings stemming from our childhoods which meant the issue of having a child was emotionally problematic. We were also all feminists and striving to build our careers in a man's world. At that time (the 1970s and 1980s), it felt like women had to choose: career or baby. It seemed almost impossible to have both. We had seen our mothers underachieve in their own lives, being reluctant mothers and feeling incomplete women as a consequence. We were not going to make similar mistakes. The only problem was that by rebelling we were possibly going to do ourselves out of the joy of procreating.

At first this seemed tolerable, but as each of us got to the age of thirty-five, moving towards forty, it became an extremely painful issue to wrestle with. Baby *or* career? Baby *and* career? How many women did we know who had done both successfully and not lost their hard-won career opportunities or their sense of self? How would we afford to have babies and at the same time be able to maintain ourselves - and our individuality - as single women, lovers and partners, artists, writers, film-makers, TV producers, translators, musicians, campaigners and teachers? Furthermore, most of us didn't feel we had the right man or kind of relationship from which a baby could stem (a common feeling among late mothers).

This was against a backdrop of motherhood being viewed as 'less than'. At that time women would say, apologetically, 'I'm just a housewife.' Being a career woman, earning money, becoming educated, were hard-won freedoms and many women who are now in their forties will have been through that particular ideological mill during their twenties and thirties.

For many women of my generation, not having a child was tantamount to a political statement. It said: 'I'm me, I'm not an appendage, or a mother, or a wife. I'm an individual.' Somewhat prophetically, we were the generation who bought 'Don't Do it, Di' badges when Lady Di was about to marry Prince Charles. We also had *Spare Rib* magazine posters pinned up which stated: *'You start off sinking into his arms and end up with your arms in his sink.'* Germaine Greer's path-breaking *The Female Eunuch* was our bible. Deciding not to have children was - and is - fine as long as it was - and is - a choice. I think for most of my adult life (up until forty) I was in rebellion and in a sense my rejection of motherhood was a reaction, rather than a real, free choice.

As the years progressed after I had turned thirty-five, the physical urge to have children got stronger and the emotional dilemmas seemed to become more and more complicated. Some of my staunch feminist friends had 'late' babies and although I volunteered childcare and other support, we eventually drifted apart. As often happens between women friends, the divide between being a mother and not being one had become too big a gap to bridge in many, though not all, cases.

I had married a man who was as ambivalent about children as I was which is why we fitted together, at least, at first. We also came from very different cultures (he was Jewish, I was Gentile), which meant we would both have to cross a cultural divide if we had children. I also believe, like many women I interviewed for this book, that my first husband was more like my son than my husband, which was something we both acknowledged towards the end of our relationship. I had a strong desire to nurture, which I turned inappropriately on my partner and friendships at the time. Looking back, I can now see I was desperate to have a baby, but couldn't really acknowledge it to myself. The can of worms was ready to burst open, and I was sitting on the lid, forcing it closed.

However, when my marriage finally foundered, the Baby Question was disturbingly still unanswered. I was thirty-eight and forty was fast approaching. I'd ended a perfectly decent ten-year marriage, to a perfectly decent man, and now I was alone. It was clear all was hopeless on the baby front (and anyway, I was still somewhat ambivalent). I even had a torrid, destructive affair with a toyboy who promised a baby - an empty promise, as it turned out - which ended in tears.

As my mid-life crisis deepened, I got into Jungian therapy, something for which I will always be grateful. By sheer luck, I was recommended to an absolutely superb therapist, who was wise, mature and strong enough to help me. I went to her, desperate and distraught about the unsolved Baby Question, and I truly believe she was the real midwife not only to my true self, but to my baby. Without entering therapy I think I would have spent the rest of my life wondering 'What if?', 'Should I have ... ?' and 'If only...' It would have been like that tragically funny cartoon, in which the fifty-year-old wakes up and says, 'Oh, my God, I forgot to have children.' I now believe that would have been the biggest tragedy of my life, far bigger than any ten-ton lorry trying to crush me to death.

Then something strange happened. I was living alone in my house in North London, struggling to write my first book, *Off the Hook* (now published as *Overcoming Addiction* by Piatkus), and a cat moved in. I had always been allergic to cats and so I spent much of the summer pushing the mog out the back door. However, he would scoot past me and settle on a chair, looking rather beautiful. The biggest thing that worried me about cats (apart from the fleas and my allergy), was the issue of *dependency*. There was I, shedding husbands and lovers and deciding never to have children and whoosh a cat turns up, literally, on the mat. No, I definitely didn't want to have a cat. I spent a few weeks resisting until, one day, the milk I had put down for the hedgehogs which roamed the garden at night was scoffed by the cat. The turning point was buying my first tin of cat food. Cursing, I found myself opening the tin. 'I can't be doing this,' I told amused friends and later I told my Babies Group, 'It's like having a baby.' Then I bought a cat flap and actually paid for someone to insert it in the back door. I was definitely heading for middle-aged 'catdom' of the spinster kind.

However, the coming of the cat (who soon velcroed himself to me night and day, sleeping on my chest, in my bed, and sitting on my lap as I wrote, head perched on my writing hand, hobbling up and down as I struck the keypad) heralded the coming of a new man into my life and, finally, a baby at forty plus.

I didn't want a new man in my life any more than I'd wanted a cat. But I met him, quite inadvertently, in a comedy club late one night after I'd written chapter one of *Off the Hook*. I'd been invited along to the venue by someone I'd appeared with on a TV show, five months earlier. I don't even go to comedy clubs, and had never been to one before, yet I went alone late one night and spotted a tall, striking, red-haired man at the back of the venue. Not my type at all, but he was in a group attached to my TV contact, so I went marching up and started spouting German at him (I assumed he was a German - he actually looked like a Viking of sorts). It turned out that he was a neighbour and I noted him down as an attractive, intelligent, interesting person I'd like to make friends with after the book was finished.

Rufus turned up on my doorstep a couple of weeks later (like the cat) while I was hosting a women writers' group and we agreed to meet later that night. Thus began a tempestuous fascination which was to turn into a feisty new friendship, later a love relationship, and finally a marriage and solid partnership, sharing parenthood. There was a seven-year age difference between us and he was younger than me - something I found many late mothers share in common is having a partnership with a younger man. Like many men, he felt he had plenty of time on his hands. Children would be had later, much later. However, he was tangling with a forty-year-old who had the biological clock not only ticking, but dinning, in her ears. One thing was clear: he, unlike my first husband, really wanted children and in one of our late-night heart-to-hearts, he movingly confessed he felt his life would not be complete without them. We decided to live together and fairly rapidly decided to try for a child. To me, this was like jumping off a high-rise building without a bungee rope - what the hell was I doing? I'd spent all of my life desperately trying NOT to get pregnant - and now I was desperately trying TO get pregnant. Life was absurd. Damn that cat.

Being a writer, I rushed to the bookshops. Where were all the books which would guide me through this unchartered territory? I grabbed the Kitzingers and Stoppards and was amazed to find only a few lines on women my age. All the do's and don't's were fine - I gobbled down any folic acid daily, cut back my wine intake and ate plenty of fruit and veg - but there was nothing to prepare me for issues pertaining to my age. What was worse, was that all the books spoke about women being positively geriatric after the age of thirty-five. I remembered having a well-woman check at thirty-three and being told to come back pregnant as soon as possible, before it was 'too late'. Too late at thirty-three? Imagine how I felt at forty, rapidly approaching forty-one, to be bonking for baby for the first time in my life.

I did the sensible thing: I went to see my GP for advice. She didn't so much as bother to look up from the wadge of notes as she mumbled, 'I wouldn't bother if I were you.' Enraged, I wrote an article for the then *She* magazine about the rights of older and disabled women to have children. I began to see one of the obstacles which I might have to overcome was the attitude of the medical profession towards me, regarding not only age and time limits, but also disability. Through a fellow journalist, Mukti Jain Campion, who wrote a wonderfully inspiring handbook called *The Baby Challenge* (Routledge), which explains how women with physical disabilities can successfully have babies, I was given the name of Mr Anthony Silverstone at University College Hospital, London. My obstructive GP refused to refer me, so I visited the Marie Stopes Clinic in central London privately, and got them to refer me to Mr Silverstone for a pelvic examination. I really needed to know whether, as I had been told after my road accident, it was still true that I physically couldn't have children. This was fairly crucial, as I was at long last actually trying to have one.

Anthony Silverstone is my hero. He is calm, intelligent, positive, vastly knowledgeable, and yet not in the least condescending. He examined me carefully, sensitively and with great respect and simply said: 'Of course you can get pregnant.' All my fears about my pelvis and spine, my abdominal scarring, rare blood group and asthma melted into nothingness. He told me there were, of course, risks such as Down's syndrome and other disorders due to my age, and that I probably, though not necessarily, would have to have a Caesarian. Finally, he smiled sweetly at me and simply said, 'Come back when you're pregnant.'

All the staff I met at UCH had a similar attitude: positive, encouraging, hopeful, informative and concerned. I never felt patronised, I always felt included. I was listened to carefully and advised sensitively. Staff knocked on doors when they came in (even in the middle of the night) and while my disabilities were taken into account, they were never perceived to be serious obstacles to motherhood. I feel I had my baby at the right time and most definitely in the right place, because I am convinced that twenty years ago not only attitudes but also treatment would have been completely different.

It took me seven months to get pregnant. The books I read informed me that it would take me a year, maybe two. In fact, it took just seven months. It was a wonderful experience having sex without contraception for the first time in my life. It was lovely to be spontaneous and completely free. I can remember the time I actually conceived as a wondrously joyful and loving moment, bathed in sunshine. Of course, I have never before paid such close attention to my cycle. Friends regaled me with tales of taking their temperatures daily and comically putting their legs up in the air after sex in order to conceive - and now it was my turn. I felt both scared and excited. We had set off on a journey together and had no idea where or how it would end. All I knew was that finally I was throwing all caution to the wind and it felt great. Even if I never had a child, it would feel good to have tried.

I remember walking round the pond in the centre of Regent's Park and looking at all the ducks. I suddenly realised there were lots of different ducks. They were all ducks, but there were many different species, shapes, colours and sizes. I felt like a different duck - being disabled and older - and yet I was still a duck, and I had a right to have my own duckling, just like any other duck on the pond. I think my disabilities had left me with a deep-seated feeling of being different from other people and therefore not as good or as able. I had been born with talipes, a club foot, and luckily had been treated successfully as a baby at Great Ormond Street Hospital. I think this had left some sort of lasting impression upon me psychologically, that I was not 'normal', a feeling probably compounded by the fact that I also spent a long time in an incubator and was separated at birth from my mother. I also had lost my twin when my mother was five months pregnant and so I was left with all sorts of mixed and complex emotions.

However, when I finally saw the thin blue line appear on my pregnancy test, it was the most wonderful moment in my life. I felt truly female, truly human at last. Some internal taboo had been broken. I was utterly and completely thrilled. I sat in the garden in the afternoon spring sunshine on 25 April 1996, just grinning. When Rufus came home, he leapt in the air and whooped for joy, before sitting down next to me on the grass, grinning too. Even Splat the cat looked ridiculously happy as he stretched out in the sun. Rufus was thirty-five, I was forty-two and we were parents-to-be.

I drank a lot of ginger beer over the next three months. I felt almost permanently nauseous and quivery. But I was regularly scanned and monitored by UCH and I felt well, except for feeling ravenous and exhausted all the time. The pregnancy was relatively uneventful and the baby was due at Christmas, 1996.

After some serious thought, we decided to have an amniocentesis and that was definitely a very tense time. The nuchal folds scan, which measures the baby's neck and is an early indicator of Down's and other abnormalities, had been normal, but my 'double test' (a blood test to screen for disability risk) had been very high (it's weighted for age). Being a journalist, I did my research and asserted my rights. I wanted the very best person to do the amniocentesis test and was lucky that Professor Roden at University College Hospital was available. I had discovered from my research that manual skill and experience is crucial to success. Even with the best treatment, I began to feel strangely wobbly inside after the test was done and, fearing a miscarriage, the hospital admitted me for the night.

At 4.00 a.m., watching the baby's strong pulsing heartbeat on a monitor, Rufus and I realised how much we already loved our child and how desperate we were to keep it. With a pang, we both realised that we were already in love with 'Sweetpee' as we had nicknamed our progeny (a play on our surnames, Sweet and Potter). We were utterly relieved when a pale dawn arrived along with the news that I was not going to miscarry. However, the wait for the test results was almost unbearable. Having been a staunch campaigner for abortion on demand in the past, I had no idea how I would really react should I be told that the baby was disabled in any way.

Then the oddest thing happened. About five days before the test result was due I was eating a pizza, sitting in my car in a car park off the North Circular Road. This was a typical experience - sudden pangs of hunger and the desperate urge for something specific to eat. I was on my way to Brent Cross shopping centre and I'd veered off the road to satisfy my craving. I didn't have my mobile phone with me, but I suddenly had an irresistible desire to go home. It was as if I'd received a message impelling me to rush back.

I arrived much earlier than expected (we both worked at home) and asked a surprised Rufus, 'Has the hospital called?' as I came in the door. He looked perplexed, I was clearly mad with pregnancy anxiety. Then, as I entered the kitchen, the phone rang. It was the hospital, giving me my amniocentesis test results - *five days early.* I hadn't even taken my coat off. I think the midwife must have thought I was crazy because I asked her when she had decided to call me and she said she'd be reviewing my case at exactly the time I'd been sitting eating pizza in the car park. It was now 1.30 p.m. I held my breath and could hardly hear as she said: 'Good news - the baby's fine.' 'What is it?' I asked, desperate to know. We were convinced it was a boy. 'It's a girl,' she said. *I was having a baby girl. She was fine.* It was the most amazing thing I had ever experienced - I was going to have a daughter. *My daughter. Our daughter.* I cried for joy. I will never understand what happened in that car park, but I knew I had to go home, right that minute. And I'm so glad I did.

Towards the end of the pregnancy I had hypertension and then just before the birth I got terrible bronchitis (always my weakness - my lungs are a barometer of my emotional state. The worse they are, the more terrified I usually am). Rashly, we had decided to marry when I was seven months pregnant. We had a wonderful wedding in North London and honeymooned in the New Forest and Paris. It was exhausting, but it felt absolutely the right thing to do. We wanted our much-longed-for baby to be born into a secure, loving family. Marriage felt right, especially the second time around for me. We spent Christmas Day propped up in bed eating mince pies and watching *Casablanca* on TV. A strange nativity scene, with both Rufus and I sporting streaming noses and me coughing like a maniac. I remember writing a long, poignant diary entry about the imminent birth of my beloved daughter. We had named her Clara, after my late and much-loved paternal grandma. I would sing to the baby in the bath and Rufus had been talking to the bump in bed for months after the amniocentesis. She would whirl around in my abdomen (I called it 'wurzling'), responding to music and voice sounds - we already had bonded deeply before she arrived in the outside world. Even the cat would sit on my wriggling bump and purr and, not surprisingly, Clara and Splat had a very special relationship after that.

My baby was my secret treasure, and I was sad that our journey together would soon be ended. Other mothers have told me of the grief they have felt losing their babies through birth. There can be a wonderful feeling of completeness and fullness, having a baby snuggled up inside you. Regardless of backache and haemorrhoids, constant trips to the loo and the inability to breathe, sleep or eat properly, I was deeply attached to my baby and somewhat tremulous about the actual process of giving birth, albeit through a Caesarian.

Rufus and I had followed the progress of Clara's development in various birth books each week. 'Oh, she's got eyes now' or 'Wow, the spleen's developed this week.' However, the books only touched upon issues pertaining to older mothers, so it was difficult to work out what was really going to happen to me. For instance, it is common knowledge among professionals that older uteruses and pelvises can find it hard to push out a baby. But this was not really mentioned. The books all talked about the stages of labour as if all mothers were the same.

I had a last minute panic about trying to have a natural birth. Suddenly I felt I was letting my baby down by booking a Caesarian, and that if I were a real mother, I'd go the whole hog. I saw an orthopaedic consultant who examined me and said yes, it was possible - in theory - for me to give birth naturally. But Anthony Silverstone quelled my fears by calmly saying it would probably distress the baby far too much as my pelvis might not be able to function properly. He advised that I should stick to having a Caesarian. I was soothed by his advice, as I had nonetheless found myself being sucked into feeling 'less than' as a mother, unable to give birth 'properly'. Of course, in the end, what mattered more was that my child would be delivered alive and well. The focus on having the perfect birth was really a distraction from the main issue in hand.

Rufus and I had been to an NCT (National Childbirth Trust) class. Many people had recommended the classes to me and, indeed, not only was it useful to meet other prospective parents locally, but we also learned a great deal about pregnancy. However, it did not really meet my needs in two main ways: first, I was the oldest in the class, probably by eight years or so. I was definitely the only mother over forty, although some fathers were nearing my age. Second, I knew all along that I was probably going to have a Caesarian. The class was almost entirely focused on giving birth, so all the panting and pushing, puffing and screaming rehearsals were not going to help me one jot when the great moment came. The teacher was great, and tried to include me on both fronts, but I still came away feeling somewhat unprepared for the kind of birth I was going to face: an elective Caesarian. Subsequently, I felt that parentcraft and NCT classes are so focused on the birth itself, that life after birth seems only secondary. I was primarily concerned with getting the baby out as safely as possible and then getting on with the process of being a mother. Something for which no class had even so much as begun to prepare me.

The morning of Clara's birth was bizarre. It was snowing heavily and we had a car crash on the way to the hospital. Rufus braked and the car skidded on, doing a slow-motion pirouette into two cars crossing us at a T-junction ahead. Amazingly, the two drivers got out and discovered they knew each other - old friends who hadn't met for some time. The drivers shook hands and chatted amicably as I sat in the car, holding my whirling bump, and hoping against hope that I wouldn't go into labour on the spot, which could have been fatal for both Clara and I. Desperately watching the time, I struggled out of the car and explained, as snow fell thick and fast, that I was on the way to the hospital to have my baby. 'Well,' said one of the drivers, a fairly sanguine woman, 'they're hardly going to start without you, dear.' After calmly exchanging insurance details we cruised on through the snow to the hospital.

It was an unreal experience, climbing, fully sober, on to the operating table. The staff were just inserting a needle into my trembling hand when I was told there was an emergency and we'd have to wait. Aghast, I waddled back into a side room and lay, like the proverbial beached whale, on a trolley in an operating gown. It was the longest hour of my life and, unfortunately, the saline was not dripping properly into my hand, which caused problems with my blood pressure later on.

I was duly summoned ('We're just sluicing the blood from the walls - only joking! -' said the green-gowned nurse), and I clambered yet again on to the operating table. This time it was for real. I was utterly terrified. What if it all went wrong, what if the baby died, what if I was paralysed for ever, what if the epidural didn't work? I felt a sharp sting in my spine ('don't move, or we'll paralyse you for life') and a shooting pain down one leg. I was turned on my back and fairly soon a green screen was erected. Rufus was on my right side, holding my hand. I'd been told by the male anaesthetist (who looked like a Russian ballet dancer) that he would test to make sure I was fully numb from the waist down, ready for the scalpel. When I'd had my road accident, I had surfaced, while supposedly under the anaesthetic, during a major operation to save my life. I remember being sewn up while the surgeons chatted amicably over my gaping abdomen. This had left me not only with a dread of hospitals, but also of operations. 'Can you feel this?' the anaesthetist asked jocularly, squirting me with ice-cold liquid. 'Mmm, I'm not sure, maybe,' I said, gingerly. I was really scared by now. 'Well, we cut you open five minutes ago, and you haven't screamed yet,' said the surgeon, Melanie Davies, with twinklingly humorous eyes. The spinal anaesthetic had clearly worked. I was very relieved indeed. A few seconds later - or so it seemed - a long, red, greasy object floated past my peripheral vision. *My baby. Our baby.* She was being weighed (a healthy 7 lb. 6 6z.), and then there she was, swaddled, nestling on my chest, with Rufus holding her, and the hunky anaesthetist doubling as photographer. It was bizarre. She looked completely different from what I'd imagined, and for a moment I wondered if she really was my baby. However, as we were wheeled out (she was taken away to be cleaned up), it registered that she was real, alive, born and I was now a mum. I had a post-partum haemorrhage and had to stay in the recovery room while the medics sorted out my blood pressure. But about an hour later I had my baby snuggled by my side. Within minutes, she was suckling at one of my voluminous breasts as the anaesthetist showed me how to administer my own pain relief by pressing a button which released morphine (extremely necessary post op).

The next four days in hospital went by in a haze, only punctured by tender visits from family and friends. Clara almost never slept. She was on the breast constantly and although exhausted, I became pretty adept at feeding. My theory is the Caesarian had sort of wrenched Clara out of her snuggly safe place before she was ready, and constant breastfeeding was a way of trying to replicate the umbilical cord. I was very exhausted as she fed night and day, but I fought off all attempts from well-meaning midwives to put her in a plastic cot. My own memories of being incubated made me want her by my side, close to me, where she belonged.

On the third night, a wonderful Chinese midwife saw my dilemma: I was exhausted; couldn't get any sleep, but I wanted to keep feeding and stay close to my baby. She prepared a customised nest in my narrow bed, and Clara and I sank into a deep and restful sleep for over five hours. Our first proper sleep together since she was born. We barely moved all night. I remember waking in the morning, finally refreshed and calm, and looking down at the fine eyelashes and tiny nose and fingers, I was engulfed with what I can only describe as a perfect love. My heart soared and I found myself creating poetic lines about my newborn. Sadly; I never wrote them down, I was too gaga, but I felt my heart was healing from all sorts of past griefs. Parts of me, never before touched by the light of day, had finally opened to the sun.

To write the rest of my story would probably take up the rest of this book. So I must telescope the tale. I spent nine months being an at-home, full-time mum to Clara. I breast-fed, happily and easily, for thirteen months. Breastfeeding was wonderful and I carried a brightly coloured cushion with me everywhere, to lift Clara to the right height and therefore save my back from strain. The recovery from the Caesarian was slow and painful, and I felt exhausted a lot of the time. I had also put on lots of weight, which seemed hard to shift. But the sheer joy of having a healthy, happy baby overcame any negative aspects of the experience.

I met up with my NCT group every week and we sat, like happy, brain-dead milk machines, drinking tea and munching on biscuits, regaling each other with every single aspect of poo, piles and dripping breasts. This contact was a lifeline. We always had a laugh and I came away feeling more reassured and less isolated - even though I remained the oldest and most obviously disabled. I coined the phrase 'poo-and-paint' friends through this experience - something which denotes the kind of parental friendships your children bring into your life. No standing on ceremony, no best clothes or best behaviour. We learned to carry on blissfully while one baby would puke on the carpet and another would pee on someone's lap. It was (and still is) wonderfully reassuring to make this kind of poo-and-paint friendship.

Clara slept with us blissfully for the first six months, something I would thoroughly recommend to any prospective parent despite the fears. It was particularly useful for breastfeeding as I would simply roll her from one side

of my body to the other as she cuddled up and latched on,
while I drifted back into precious sleep. There was no getting
up in the cold of the night (and it was the dead of winter)
in my dressing gown to walk her around a room. It felt very
natural and heavenly to sleep three in a bed. Even when she
was a feisty four-year-old, those early weeks and months of
closeness have laid a foundation of love, intimacy and trust
between us which can be easily rekindled, especially when she
gets ill or just lonely. Her move into her own room felt like the
first big step towards separation, a process which continued
until she finally packed up to leave home at eighteen for Uni.

I think the whole experience of having a baby had been
such an unexpected delight to me - I was forty-three when
I had her - that I was keen to get on and have a second baby
almost immediately. Thus, nine months after her birth I
found myself pregnant again.

Clara was eating solids by now, and I had started working
again part-time. I had employed a wonderful nanny, Hayley
Baker, who would bring Clara to my office for a feed and
cuddle while she took a tea-break. Rufus and I were both
thrilled to be pregnant again, both fully grasping the reality
of my age and our time limits. We started looking forward
to the summer when the baby would be born - at least we
would have all the baby gear and there would not be too big
an age gap between the children. Yes, it would be difficult,
exhausting, painful at first but, well, we would have our
family complete by the time I was forty-four.

Alas, it was not to be and 'Splodgit' (our nickname for
the new baby) was miscarried at twelve weeks. I was utterly
devastated. Until that moment, I had never contemplated
miscarriage as a possibility, even though, statistically, I
knew the risk increased with age. My first pregnancy had
been so relatively straightforward that I had naively assumed
that everything would be fine the second time around. I felt
utterly shaken, and yet I still had to care for Clara and meet
my journalistic deadlines (I was now writing a new book and
had become Contributing Editor on *New Woman* magazine,
in Australia)

After an operation to remove the so-called 'products' of pregnancy - an ERPC (evaluation of retained products of conception, otherwise known as a 'scrape') - Rufus and I decided to try again. Within a month I was pregnant. Again it was a three-month pregnancy, but this time it was twins. I was shocked. Yes, I definitely wanted another baby - but two? Oh Lord. I didn't realise that multiple pregnancy was commonplace after forty, as ovaries can eject more than one egg a month as a last ditch attempt to get pregnant. I wrote a piece for *She* and *Woman's Realm* magazines about the experience of facing double motherhood at forty-four. However, I again miscarried at twelve weeks, first one baby, then the second. I was devastated, although somewhat relieved not to be having twins. I had another scrape. After a break of three months, we tried again and within a month I was pregnant: this time I miscarried naturally at six weeks. My next and final pregnancy lasted three months. This time I was certain that it would be absolutely fine - I was extremely pregnant. Surely I'd be fifth-time lucky? Exhausted, nauseous, ballooning, hungry, surely this time it would stay? Sadly, the baby miscarried at eleven weeks. I had my third and final op. Desperate, I had read Professor Lesley Regan's excellent book, *Miscarriage: What Every Woman Needs to Know* (Bloomsbury), and had got myself referred to her Recurrent Miscarriage Unit at St Mary's Hospital, Paddington. After extensive tests she could find nothing wrong with me and simply said what was now for me the well-worn adage, 'Come back when you're pregnant.' I was then forty-five.

The heartbreak of losing baby after baby was wearing me down, physically and emotionally. It was also taking its toll on my relationship with Rufus as each time I miscarried, I was plunged into the depths of despair and grief for weeks. Hormonally, it was a roller-coaster ride as my body tried to right itself and emotionally, I felt totally at sea.

Rufus and I reacted very differently to my miscarriages - I felt he was too aloof and distant, treating them like a visit to the dentist. He said he felt overwhelmed and upset by my level of grief. It's quite common for men and women to respond very differently to miscarriage because, after all, the event is happening inside the woman's body, affecting her emotions and hormones, even at a very early stage. Men are not thrown by hormone changes and sickness, or fantasies of a small baby suckling. It's hard for men to connect with the reality of a pregnancy at a distance. It was a difficult time for us to endure and the fact that I had been pregnant five times in just over two years was physically and mentally exhausting. I believed that if I just kept trying it would happen in the end. And indeed, had I had the luxury of another five years, I might have waited a year and then started all over again. But my age was against me.

Eventually, I had a long and helpful talk with Anthony Silverstone, Clara's obstetrician, and he put things in perspective: 'Don't miss Clara's childhood by trying endlessly for a baby you might not have.' The Miscarriage Association was also helpful and I wrote a piece on miscarriage for *She* magazine, which helped me grieve. I discovered that I was not alone and that it is incredibly common for women to miscarry. Soberingly, a woman I interviewed had miscarried ten times - and still had no baby. Then two of my closest women friends from the NCT group also miscarried (though they were ten years younger than me). Miscarriage was everywhere. The only difference being that younger women had time on their side to try again, and indeed my NCT friends both went on to have second babies.

My baby remained alone. I felt I had no other forty-plus mothers to commiserate with - until I started researching this book. Then I found many mothers my age who were dealing with the inability to have another child (or even to have one in the first place.) Most of these forty-plus mothers had had a miscarriage - or three - at some point during the process of trying to have a late child. This knowledge enabled me to begin to let go of the dream of having a second child and instead give my full attention to thoroughly enjoying my beautiful daughter.

Being an older mother meant that my career was already established and indeed thriving, and it also needed my attention. Each book I write is almost like another baby - it needs a lot of time, attention and care to bring it into the world. And in a sense, this book is like my second and final 'baby'. Clara has a mother who is constantly midwifing some book or writing project. And she experiences a certain level of sibling rivalry - albeit with my job - as a consequence. Of course, I have met many late mothers who have decided to give up their jobs in order to be with their very precious child or children. I think this is an issue that each forty-plus mother has to work out for herself. Most research points to the happiest, most well-adjusted and accomplished children having mothers who can work part-time. It also depends on the level and quality of childcare a baby gets. Clearly, competing for attention with a group too soon can damage a child emotionally. Children need a great deal of love, safety, affection, stimulation, calm, security and, of course, firm boundaries.

Our own choice - and perhaps also typical of late motherhood, class and culture - was to employ Hayley for nearly three years, at first on a part-time basis, until Clara began to go to an excellent nursery school. I am the sort of person who needed to keep her career going - the old feminist thinking had not died entirely. As a writer, I need to write. I also love broadcasting, and curbed my counselling to enable me to become a magazine and radio 'agony aunt' and life coach. Anyway, we needed the money to live - I was not exactly a woman of leisure. Working part-time for most of Clara's life has kept me sane and fulfilled and that in itself, I believe, has created a fairly happy home and child.

But that's not the end of the story. When you are a forty-plus mother, all sorts of things change. I have lost old friends, and gained new ones, for instance. Two of my closest, most trusted, friends (also in their forties) dumped me when I got pregnant and had a baby. One, who had grown-up children of her own, wrote to me saying 'I'll see you at the christening', when I told her I was pregnant. But although we spoke nearly daily before my change of status, she was not able to support me emotionally throughout my pregnancy. I was deeply hurt at the time, but understood, in retrospect, that she was used to having me available to her and was, in a sense, experiencing a kind of grown-up sibling rivalry with my new baby. The experience of losing and gaining friends over pregnancy is something many women in this book share.

Another single friend told me I had become a 'breastfeeding bore' (which I probably had), and after a couple of years cut off our friendship, without any real explanation. Again, in retrospect, I understood how painful it was for her to be a friend to someone who was having a child in middle-age - something she yearned for, but could not achieve, due to her own personal history. These losses hurt greatly, but in their place have come new, less intense, more balanced friendships. Most of my friendships today (although not all) revolve around our children - and there are plenty of fun events these days, where parents and children mix together over home-cooked meals, birthday parties, picnics and other festivities. These are true poo-and-paint friends. Gone are the days of bosom buddy best friendships which, to some extent, I feel belong to my more carefree and self-centred twenties and thirties. Part of growing up, I suppose.

Of course, there is still scope to glam up and go out for a night on the town - which I relish with good female or male friends, or with Women In Journalism, Radio or PR colleagues. I love nothing better than donning a splash of lippy and glitter, and enjoying plenty of gossip. It's essential to be myself in these social situations, just as much as when I'm writing in the solitude of my office or broadcasting in the monkish silence of a studio.

Family has also taken on a new importance and I made a real effort for Clara to meet up with her cousins, grandparents and extended family. Luckily, my cousins and sisters-in-law, who sensibly all had babies in their thirties, have children the same age as Clara. This has meant she has a network of cousins who I hope will all remain friends throughout their lives, and therefore beyond my own lifetime. Due to increased longevity and fitness, Clara's grandparents (Rufus's parents divorced and remarried, and my parents are dead) are generally a sprightly and playful lot who enjoy gardening, travel, sport, opera, reading, computers and house-beautifying with a vigour and passion which belies their years.

The notion of grandparents being armchair-ridden fogies is changing; my in-laws are hard to keep up with, with their trips by bus to Vietnam, South America, Egypt or India. One set of Clara's grandparents were even newly-weds in their sixties, and one grandmother has a new romance at seventy-three. The times are indeed a-changing, especially in relation to age and our notion of what is or is not appropriate to any particular time of life. Sadly two grandfathers have now died at time of writing.

I have learned a great deal from becoming a late mother. Not least, how little I really know. I feel I have been grounded by the experience in the most delightful way. It has put things in perspective and given me a fresh purpose. Of course, if I'd never had Clara I would not be saying any of this. But, given we only have one life to lead, I feel amazingly lucky to have been able to have at least one child before it was too late. Of course, there are moments when I worry about her being alone from her own mid-life onwards (though this would mean she would be relieved of having to care for us in old age), but there's a likelihood I will be living a long and, hopefully, productive life. It had also crossed my mind to wonder how I would deal with her cries of 'Why are you so old and wrinkly, Mummy?' when she began to realise how much older I was than her peers' mothers. But it didn't happen; I have the maturity, grace and humour to deal with any disparaging remarks from her, or anyone else. For confidence is something that also comes with age - as well as tolerance, patience, self-acceptance and self-knowledge. I think I was pretty lucky to 'get one in before closing time' and I'm certainly going to make the best of it - and the rest of my life - not only for my daughter's sake, but for my own.

2018 update:

As time and life has moved on, although Rufus and I have gone our separate ways, our bond with our precious daughter continues. In fact, now 22, my daughter has edited this book for its new e-life, something I could never have envisaged way back when.

2

Myth 1: Past it at Forty

REALITY TODAY: FORTY IS THE NEW THIRTY

'I don't look my age and I certainly don't behave like it,' was the heartfelt cry from most women interviewed for this book. 'No, I don't look forty, and in fact, most of my friends think I'm much younger than I am.'

'Looking forty' is something most of us dread: the out-of-date stereotype is a Mrs Brown-ish hairnet, grey cardigan, middle-aged spread, frumpy slippers and spectacles. Looking forty has always meant looking 'past it'. In our culture, age and the ageing process are hated with a vengeance, and reaching the watershed of forty has held a dread of heralding the beginning of the end, particularly for women. Unfairly, men are believed to ripen with age while staying sexy like the original Don Juan or today's craggy versions – the late Peter Stringfellow, Harrison Ford or Al Pacino. Furthermore, if a woman has remained unmarried or childless, she has been labelled 'on the shelf', a spinster, dowdy, in other words, useless and unattractive. Definitely past her sell-by date.

Pushing back the age boundaries

Luckily, this ghastly myth of women being 'past it at forty' is in reality just that - a myth. Forty-year-old women today, whether married, cohabiting or single - and whether mothers or not - are more physically fit, sexually active (and demanding), financially independent, career-orientated, and more fashion, appearance, and health conscious than ever before. Think of Madonna, Jerry Hall, Chrissie Hynde, Caroline Quentin, Emma Thompson, Ruby Wax, Iman, Cherie Blair, Cate Blanchett, Kate Winslet, Jane Seymour, and you inevitably think of women who are sexy, vibrant, intelligent, talented, powerful, successful and mature. Older celebrities, like Joan Collins, Lauren Bacall, Shirley McLaine, Zhandra Rhodes, Molly Parkin, Germaine Greer, even the Queen Mother, have done their bit in pushing back our perception of women and age. These women refused to be pigeon-holed as 'past it' not only at forty, but also at fifty, sixty, a hundred and beyond. They have not joined the ranks of beige-clad OAPs, they have revelled in the limelight and remained glamorous, creative, intelligent and socially powerful to the last.

Women Celebrities Having Babies Over Forty		
Patricia Hodge	Felicity Kendal	Annette Bening
Jenny Agutter	Emma Thompson	Melanie Griffith
Jane Seymour	Victoria Wood	Madonna
Cherie Blair	Fiona Phillips	Jerry Hall
Caroline Quentin	Lisa Hartman	Denise Welch
Susan Sarandon	Sigourney Weaver	Julie Walters
Anna Ford	Mary Quant	Koo Stark
Sally Thomsett	Maeve Haran	Maureen Freely
Louise Chunn	Yvonne Roberts	

Of course, men technically can carry on having babies until they die, because all they have to produce is sperm. Male celebrities have also been leading the way, having babies later in life, often with younger women, but not always. This is often due to wanting to seal a second or third marriage or partnership with a baby, and also a way of 'proving' their ongoing virility and youthful attractiveness.

Male Celebrities Having Babies Over Forty
• Al Pacino (60) - having a baby with his 48-year-old partner, Beverley D'angelo, through IVF
• The late David Bowie (53) - had baby, Zahra, with model Iman (45)
• Ben Elton (41) - having twins, through IVF, with Sophie (33)
• David Jason (61) - having a baby with his 41-year-old partner
• Tony Blair (46) - had baby Leo with Cherie (45)
• Michael Douglas (55) - had baby Dylan with Catherine Zeta, Jones (30)
• John Humphrys (57) - had a baby with his 42-year-old partner
• Mick Jagger (56) - late babies with Jerry Hall (41), and with Luciana Morad (30)
• Warren Beatty (56) - with Annette Bening (43)
• Phil Collins (49) - with second wife Orianne (28)
• James Doohan (*Star Trek's* Scotty) (80) - with Wende (43)

Breaking out of the 'doll's house'

The knock-on effect of these celebrity role models has been to give hope to women of all ages that it is not too late to do what they want with their lives - whatever their age. The nineteenth-century playwright, Henrik Ibsen, wrote the path-breaking stage play *The Doll's House* about a woman, Nora, wanting to break out of the confines of her assigned role of wife and mother. This was reflected in the Suffragette movement which fought for fifty years for women to get the vote (only granted to all women in the UK in 1928). From the mid-twentieth century onwards, women in the Women's Liberation Movement again began to push back the boundaries of their restrictive roles primarily as daughters and housewives. In post-war Britain, women were supposed to be satisfied with being decorative while keeping house and having babies. Few had the opportunity to travel, or to be educated, financially independent, sexually free or to work. Indeed, once they had become mothers, women were usually forced to give up work by their employers and husbands. As in *The Doll's House*, women went from their father's house to their husband's, with no chance in between to explore themselves, life or the world.

Greater freedom, greater choices

However, this has changed radically today. The Women's Liberation Movement has been highly successful in helping women not only change their perception of themselves, but also make demands on employers, partners/husbands and, of course, the law.

Today, most women expect to be financially independent and to have a significant job or career from school onwards. Indeed, there is so much onus on women being independent, that some women are now choosing *not* to work if and when they have children. Some highly successful women who have made it to the top (like businesswoman Nicola Horlick) have stepped down to work part-time because they want to put their families first.

It seems as if we have come full circle, with women returning to the hearth. But it isn't exactly the case, as women now have a *choice*. Fifty years ago there was no choice; today, women have a variety of choices available to them in a variety of ways. Clearly, the more educated women are, the greater the choices and freedoms they will enjoy.

Through the use of the Pill (and morning-after pill, now available over the counter), women can control their fertility. The consequence of this has been that women can choose when, where and how they have children - something which was generally unthinkable before the 1960s. More women are able to combine motherhood with work than ever before (most married women work), and thus, having a baby is no longer viewed as the end of a woman's career.

'There is something so heavenly about your own baby... looking back, I think I was probably a bit of a workaholic. But when I became pregnant, I was forced to take some time off. I thought I wouldn't be able to cope [with being a mother] but I was wrong as it's been really enjoyable. I was terrible when I was pregnant. Once I put a mobile phone in the fridge and left it overnight. But that's the wonderful thing about pregnancy - it gives you licence to be a lunatic. I love it. I'm hoping to be just as mad the second time around.'

Caroline Quentin, 41-year-old actress, on motherhood, quoted in *Now* magazine, 2000

(Caroline sadly miscarried her second baby, but then gave birth again in 2003)

Through its National Childcare Strategy, the Government is currently improving maternity and paternity benefits, as well as employment practices, to encourage women to stay with their jobs after giving birth. Women in their twenties today think nothing of putting off having babies until their thirties, even forties, as a consequence. In the not too distant future, they may well choose to freeze their eggs in their early twenties and 'bank' them until they are ready later - much later - and when the time is right to have a child. This could be in their thirties, forties, even fifties or sixties, and it could be done alone or in a loving partnership.

Birth begins at forty

We used to say, 'life begins at forty', to cheer up women perched on the edge of serious middle age. To a significant minority of women we can now say, 'birth begins at forty', as some women are choosing to have their babies in their early, mid- or late, forties, or even beyond into their fifties (like Lynne Bezant, below). Technology has advanced in leaps and bounds since Louise Brown was the first controversial test-tube baby in 1978. In Vitro Fertilisation (IVF) and associated technology has become big business and has opened the doors to parenthood for women who, twenty years ago, would have given up trying. Today, egg donation is a popular way for older women to have babies.

Twins at Fifty-Six

Lynne Bezant (56) and her husband Derek are poised to be the oldest couple in Britain to have twins using IVF at time of writing. They already have three children who have left home (26, 30 and 32). Lynne had already gone through the menopause and Derek had had a vasectomy. Although controversy raged over whether they should be allowed to have babies at their age due to their fitness, health and probable complications during birth, they were completely within the law in having private embryological treatment at the London Gynaecological Clinic in Harley Street. Dr Charlie Lewis, Professor of Psychology at Lancaster University said of the Bezants in a Mirror article (22 January 2001): 'There are many advantages to being older parents. First, they have got wisdom and experience that younger parents haven't got. And these parents are probably more financially secure than they were when they brought up their first set of kids. The main problem I see ahead is the issue of life expectancy.'

This trend of having babies later in one's life was unthinkable in the 1960s and 1970s, when most women had their first babies at twenty-one. Even having a baby at thirty was seen as extraordinary back then. 'In the early 1980s, when women had their babies in their late twenties, we called a woman of thirty an "elderly prima gravida" which meant she was "old" regarding childbearing,' explains Julia Berryman, ex-Senior Lecturer in Psychology at Leicester University and head of its Parenthood Research Group. However, 'Our view of what a woman is like at forty has changed dramatically over the past thirty years,' she says. In the twenty-first century, women are generally having their babies later - the average age of a woman having her first child now being about thirty. This means the benchmark of being 'old' for childbearing has shifted to thirty-five, and is gradually edging up to thirty-seven in the eyes of the medical profession. The Royal College of Obstetricians advises women to think of 27 as the optimum time for having a baby – something many 20-plus women would baulk at as far too early today. There is more information, knowledge and technological help than ever before to help women have their babies successfully. And this is especially true for women who are having babies late - or who had even given up all hope of having them at all.

Jane's story: having a baby at fifty

Jane, now fifty-four, had a baby boy when she was fifty, having given up all hope of ever having a child. Her story exemplifies how our perception of women's age has changed and how medical and technological progress has made the impossible possible.

'I was married for nine years to my first husband and although I didn't really want children with him, I got pregnant when I was thirty-three. The doctor put a stitch in my cervix because it was thought I might miscarry. But I wasn't given any advice about what I should or shouldn't be doing. I started bleeding and had to sit in a hospital bed for five weeks. I was very scared, and then I began to miscarry the baby through the cervical stitch. They wouldn't call the doctor, the nurse just said, "You'll be all right, you're not in that much pain." But I was, it was agony. I kept pleading with her to get the doctor, and she just kept saying "You'll be all right." I wasn't. The baby - which was five months old by then - tore my cervix to shreds as it miscarried. It was utterly traumatic because I saw the baby when he was born and he was still breathing. My husband wasn't with me - he was a keen sailor, and was off doing his sporty activities. He didn't want to be around all that squeamish women's stuff. He didn't lend me any support at the time - I don't think we really expected men to be involved that much back then.

'Anyway, two things happened then. I had a dilation and curettage (d. and c.) at the hospital, but they didn't do it properly. I eventually saw a private Harley Street doctor who was utterly appalled at my condition. He said it was a "butcher's job" and he had to cut away part of my cervix which had been damaged by the birth. Then I found out I had abnormal cells -I had got cervical cancer. I had a biopsy and they took more of the cervix away. I was told I wouldn't conceive again and therefore would not be able to have children. My marriage went downhill from there. I think the death of our baby acted as a catalyst to the marriage breakup. I realised having a baby with a man like my husband would have been disastrous. He wanted me to be his mum, really. When I needed support, I didn't see him for dust. So, six months after the miscarriage, I left him.

'At this point, I felt sure I would never have a child. I started up a travel business which turned out to be very successful. I suppose I threw myself into it because I needed to rebuild my life and confidence. I worked at it for fifteen years and made a lot of money. During this time I had a few relationships, but nothing really serious. Then I met Tim in 1993. I met him at a party and we chatted, but I didn't really fancy him. I thought, "Not bad looking, intelligent, but far too young for me." He pursued me after the party, but I thought he was mad. He's ten years younger than me and to be honest, I didn't take the relationship seriously. I thought the age gap was too great and it was really a toyboy affair that just kept going. Ironically, he had been thinking about having children, but I said, "Look, one of the drawbacks to us going further is that I'm too old to have children, plus I've got physical problems which would make it impossible." I told him, "You'd better find yourself a younger person to have your family with." But he just smiled at me and said, "I love you. Let's see what we can do." I was flabbergasted. We started living together. I didn't expect anything to happen, but I had some injections to stimulate my ovaries, and then went through private hormone treatment and my eggs were removed, fertilised by Tim's sperm in a lab, grown in a dish, and then three embryos were implanted. And bingo, I became pregnant at fifty years of age. I couldn't believe it because I'd been told categorically I'd never, ever be able to have a baby. I had another cervical stitch put in, again privately. The gynaecologist said my cervix was a real mess, but he worked at repairing it for two hours. Afterwards, I felt like I'd been strung up - the whole of my lower half felt like it had been tied up in knots and pulled tight. It made my uterus feel like Fort Knox.

'In preparation for the birth, I sold my business. My consultant said, "Entomb yourself if you want this baby, you can't do anything. No sex, no exercise, no nothing." I was a fit woman, I loved skiing, going to the gym, swimming, cycling. I ate sensibly, didn't smoke, but had the occasional glass of wine. I definitely was fitter than your average fifty-year-old, but nonetheless I was told to watch it. I found this extremely hard. I didn't walk anywhere, I didn't exercise during the whole pregnancy, but ultimately it was worth it. I had the nuchal folds scan [which measures the baby's neck] for abnormalities at twelve weeks and the consultant said he thought it all looked fine. Tim and I decided against an amniocentesis because I didn't want to risk a miscarriage. I guess I felt this was my one and only chance, and I really wanted this baby, no matter what.

'The pregnancy went remarkably well. I got worried at twenty weeks - because that was when I had miscarried the last time. I had a scare when I started bleeding and I went into hospital. They said that one of the stitches had broken with the weight of the baby, but that everything was fine. It was a horrendously tense time. But this time I wasn't alone, because Tim was there, holding my hand, being very supportive, utterly unlike my first husband. At thirty-eight weeks I had an elective Caesarian. I was given a course of steroids from twenty-four to thirty weeks, to help the baby's lungs mature (I think this was an insurance against early birth, so the baby could breathe and survive). They also took the remaining stitches out of my cervix, so that if I went into labour early, I wouldn't harm the baby.

'I did a bit of light office work during the last weeks of the pregnancy, simply because I needed to keep my mind occupied. I had invested the money I had made from selling my business, so we had no money problems (also my partner earns well). It was a tense time, waiting, but we got there eventually. I found the attitude of the hospital staff (NHS) extremely kind and helpful and totally different from when I'd had my first miscarriage, seventeen years earlier. The consultant was also extremely thoughtful. He took a personal interest, I think due partly to my age, and partly to my medical history. I had a spinal anaesthetic and was soon holding a perfect baby boy, 7 lb. 5 oz. in weight. I'd been convinced the baby was a girl and we hadn't thought up any boy's names. Tim was there throughout, of course, and we were elated - I can't describe how happy I was.

'Tim took a week off work and my mother-in-law came to stay for a few days. I breastfed, but it was difficult. The baby didn't sleep much, so I took him for cranial osteopathy and he settled down after that. I felt very exhausted those first few weeks, but very, very happy. He slept in our room for the first three weeks and then we put him in his own room nearby, so I could get some sleep.

'Being a full-time mum took some adapting to, especially at my age. I did go back to work at six months, for two days a week, but soon decided I felt too split between work and motherhood. I'm now at home full-time with Andy, although I have started doing a psychology diploma. I come from a tough background and in fact, my mother and sisters were very negative about me having a baby late in life. My mother said I was barking mad and wondered "what the hell was I doing it for at my time of life?" My mother has subsequently died and my sisters and I are wrangling over the Will. This means the baby has no maternal grandmother (in fact, she disinherited him because she didn't approve of me getting pregnant late). One of my younger sisters, who has two kids, is a bit of a queen bee and I think she felt envious of me and worried she would get knocked off her perch. She said she'd rather have needles stuck in her eyes, than ever see me again. This caused me quite a lot of distress and I did go for some counselling as a consequence. However, I've become very interested in psychology after all this, and studying it is also helping me understand my family (and of course, the baby's development) more.

'Of course, there is a big age gap between me and the other mothers I meet locally, but I've made new friends with some of them. At first I found it hard *just* being a mum after working all my life. I found I wasn't being stimulated, as I was used to running my own business and I felt a bit cut off. However, at four, Andy's now in a private kindergarten and he's making friends (and so am I). He mixes well with other children, and he's a very sociable, gorgeous little chap. I want to bring him up to be a well-balanced, friendly child, who has a good relationship with his peers. I know my energy levels aren't what they were in my twenties and thirties, but I'm still reasonably fit, and my tolerance and patience levels are a lot higher than they would have been earlier in my life. I would have loved Andy to have siblings, but I don't think that's on as I started the menopause soon after the birth, and am now on HRT. We've thought about adopting, but my age is an enormous drawback.

'However, I feel so extremely pleased to have had my own child - no matter how late. I feel incredibly lucky because my life has opened up, it's been enriched immeasurably and it's put me in touch with bits of me that were dormant before. I'm lucky I'm with a partner whom I adore, we have an easy relationship and a lovely son to boot. I simply love being an older mother and I think he feels this. Having a baby at fifty has been a tremendous bonus to me, especially when I'd lost the chance of ever having a family at all. Tim and I married when our son was two, and I feel we're together for life. I want him to be his own man and to give him the best loving, caring start in life we possibly can.'

The risks over forty

Of course, Jane's story is a rare case, because few women go on to have babies at fifty. However, it is a strong example of how women's lives have changed for the better over the past thirty years. Not only have medical advances meant that women like Jane can have a late baby, despite physical difficulties, but also that the changes in our ideas about relationships meant she could move on to be with a man who was much younger than she was, and a proactive father. She had also earned and saved money in her own right, and so was not dependent on her partner for money, either for treatment or living. This picture is so different from the stories our mothers and grandmothers would tell about their lack of choice, hardship, staying with one man for life (whether the marriage was loveless or violent or childless). Jane endures envy from family members (something many successful mothers over forty experience - as well as from friends), because she has managed to 'have it all' in a very contemporary way.

However, it is essential not to gloss over the risks involved in trying for a baby over forty. These are very real and must be faced by any woman trying for children in her forties. Of course, each woman - and therefore each case - must be looked at individually. Which is why it is crucial to try and ascertain a profile of your own gynaecological health before you start trying for a baby. This can be done by visiting a specialist Well Woman clinic and having tests to see if you are still ovulating, for starters.

Infertility

Generally, fertility begins to drop at around twenty-seven, and reduces increasingly from thirty-five, and thus many women may find it harder to conceive after forty. It is not unusual for an older woman to 'try' for a baby for a year, even two, before she conceives. As women near the menopause and become 'peri-menopausal', their periods can become erratic as their ovaries age. This can lead to periods being missed altogether in months where no ovulation occurs. This can create infertility, which is a highly distressing experience for women trying to get pregnant.

Age clearly plays an important part. 'Infertility patients tend to be older and chromosomal abnormalities in the baby increase with advancing maternal age,' explains Professor Lesley Regan. A study in Italy showed that in women aged forty years and older, genetic abnormalities were present in 83 per cent of the miscarriages (*Miscarriage: What Every Woman Needs to Know*, Lesley Regan, p. 165).

Delaying a first pregnancy also increases the risk of ovulatory disorders, endometriosis, fibroids and other conditions. 'The womb lining becomes progressively less suitable for the implantation of an embryo and thus places the pregnancy at greater risk,' says Professor Regan.

However, fertility treatment is a fast-growing field and in time, the technology may be in place to counter many of these negative aspects of ageing. Certainly, several women interviewed for this book had been written off due to endometriosis, fibroids and other conditions and then, having had corrective operations or treatment, and/or with the help of ovary stimulating substances such as clomid, were able not only to get pregnant, but to carry one, two or more babies to term while being over forty themselves.

There are many ways to boost fertility, such as using acupuncture, acupressure, homoeopathy and other alternative health remedies. A healthy diet, low in fat, high in fibre and complex carbohydrates, fresh fruit and vegetables (five portions a day), and no cigarettes and limited alcohol (one or two units a week), should help to boost fertility. Moderate aerobic exercise is also essential. Women should not crash diet as this can stop periods and foil their ability to get pregnant. Dietary mineral and vitamin supplements may be advised by a pharmacist, but it is essential that 100 milligrams of folic acid is taken daily, to guard against spina bifida should pregnancy occur (a lot of multivitamins contain folic acid). Of course, limiting stress while increasing resting and relaxation can also aid fertility as sustained tension puts the whole body under strain, including the fallopian tubes (which can close when stressed, limiting the possibility of conception).

Accidental pregnancy

Some women interviewed for this book spoke of throwing away their contraception for four or five, even ten, years and then suddenly getting pregnant at forty plus. It seems ovaries can start ejecting eggs furiously as a woman ages, which can create a surge in fertility as the menopause looms into view. A woman may have forgotten all about contraception in her early forties, only to find herself suddenly pregnant at forty-five, or even later. According to Julia Berryman, 'We [and the medical profession] tend to suppose women are no longer fertile after forty. Yet, surprisingly, there are as many abortions a year - about seventy to eighty - to women over fifty as there are to women under sixteen.' This results from so many women having 'accidental' pregnancies in their forties, even fifties.

As periods begin to become more erratic as the menopause approaches, it is possible for women to think they will not conceive. Yet, instead of one egg being released at ovulation time (about mid-cycle), one or two (or more) eggs may be released during a month. This can mean there is no actual 'safe' period - hence accidental pregnancy occurs if the woman is using the 'rhythm method' (avoiding intercourse during ovulation) or only using contraception during ovulation. The point being that there is a risk to health if women give up using contraception forty plus, thinking their chances of having a baby are nil. The body is in flux and therefore there is always a possibility of pregnancy. Only women who want to risk having a baby should be contraception-free until the menopause is completed.

Multiple pregnancy

Another risk is the possibility of multiple pregnancy in older women. If more than one egg is released a month it also increases the risk of multiple pregnancy. Also according to Professor Lesley Regan, in her book *Miscarriage: What Every Woman Needs to Know*, 'Many pregnancies start with more than one pregnancy sac in the uterus and many potential twins and triplets are miscarried very early. Indeed, some doctors think that as many as two-thirds of twin sacs seen on the scan during the first eight weeks 'vanish' and result in a single baby being born.'

However, if women over forty are trying to conceive and resort to fertility treatment, this can increase the incidence of a multiple pregnancy. Professor Regan explains, 'When fertility drugs are used, the number of multiple pregnancies is much higher'. This can lead to a nasty shock if a woman only wanted one more baby and ends up with two or three. It also increases the health risks, as carrying more than one foetus puts a strain on the heart, spine, lungs and endocrine system. There is an increased risk of miscarriage with an increased number of foetuses carried. Professor Regan warns, 'There is a much higher risk of early and late miscarriage, stillbirth, and an inevitable risk of premature delivery, not to mention long-term complications of being born too early... I cannot overstate the importance of ensuring that fertility treatment does not result in multiple pregnancy of triplets or more.'

Down's syndrome and other abnormalities

Having a Down's baby can be a big fear for older parents. Down's is caused by the foetus having an extra chromosome. The risk level for a woman in her twenties is only 1 in 1,500; in her thirties it is 1 in 750. By the late thirties it becomes 1 in 380, rising to 1 in 100 after 40, and 1 in 40 after the age of forty-five. Interestingly, because tests like amniocentesis and CVS (chorionic-villi sampling), which look for chromosomal abnormality in a foetus, are offered automatically to women thirty-five plus, the majority of Down's babies today are actually born to women under thirty-five. In a sense, we automatically link age with Down's, but Down's and other chromosomal abnormalities are possible at any age and, as a consequence, there are moves afoot within health authorities to offer testing to all women, regardless of age.

Screening is becoming more sophisticated and less invasive as a new blood test may be available in the future to screen for Down's early in pregnancy, avoiding the miscarriage risks associated with amniocentesis (the new procedure is still undergoing research). The introduction of a blood test would mean that forty-plus women probably would be even less likely to give birth to Down's babies. However, other chromosomally abnormal babies would still need specific screening, possibly through amniocentesis and nuchal folds scans. Screening is usually taken up by forty-plus women because of the risks involved.

Miscarriage

There is also an increased risk of miscarriage over forty. This is often due to eggs being older and therefore possibly damaged. 'For women over the age of forty, the figure is about 25 per cent - one in four,' explains Professor Lesley Regan, 'whereas, for younger women with no previous history of miscarriage, and no medical problems, the risk of miscarriage may be as low as 5 per cent.'

The body usually miscarries a foetus as a natural way of protecting against having a defective birth. However, miscarriage rates, regardless of age, are much higher than are popularly understood. Miscarriages can occur to one in three pregnancies, and to women in their teens, twenties, thirties, as well as forties. Most miscarriages occur so early in pregnancy that they may go undetected and be experienced just as a particularly heavy period. There may also be hormonal reasons for miscarriage and early detection of hormonal deficiency can help save an otherwise risky pregnancy, as a woman may be given hormone injections to sustain the pregnancy.

New research by Professor Regan is proving encouraging for many women suffering with a condition called 'anti-phospholipid antibody syndrome'. Up to 20 per cent of women who experience recurrent miscarriages have raised levels of antibodies called lupus anti-coagulants. These antibodies circulate in the blood and cause the blood vessels that supply the placenta to seize up. When this happens, the baby dies. The antibodies are diagnosed through a simple blood test. If the test is positive, the woman can be treated with low-dose aspirin or a drug called heparin, an anti-clotting agent. They can increase blood flow to the placenta, reducing clotting. However, this should always be done under a doctor's or consultant's supervision.

Aspirin Helped Me Have a Baby At Forty-four

'I have two children aged fourteen and eighteen from my first marriage. At forty-one, I remarried, and at forty-four, after several miscarriages, I had my third child, who is now two years old. While experiencing my miscarriages I was advised to take half an aspirin daily. This seemed to do the trick and a naturally occurring pregnancy followed just as time was running out. Bethany is bright and healthy and at forty-seven I am now enjoying my family.'

Lindsay, writing to me at Home & Life magazine

Emotional fallout

Even though miscarriage is a risk to a mother forty plus, she will not be alone if she has one. Women of all ages have miscarriages and it is not their fault that they do. A common misconception is that they should not have gone dancing, had sex or carried on working, and most experts say this seldom has a bearing on the outcome - if the foetus was faulty it would have aborted anyway. Nor is it a sign that the woman will not be able to conceive again. In fact, if a woman has an operation (i.e. a d. and c.) to remove the remains of the baby, this can actually help prepare the lining of the womb for a fresh pregnancy. Of course, the emotional fallout following a miscarriage is much harder to deal with and many women interviewed for this book had gone through much distress on losing a baby. Sometimes, counselling is necessary to help a woman grieve and prepare herself to try again. Physically speaking, a miscarriage should not necessarily be a barrier to further conceptions. Rather, the issue is whether the woman can bear to face a possible future loss and the subsequent distress that it may create. Encouragingly, Professor Regan's research into miscarriage shows that a woman's chance of miscarrying again is 'somewhere between 15 and 75 per cent'. It's important to bear in mind, however, that women forty plus will continue to have the higher rate of miscarriage, simply due to their age.

Julie's story: beating infertility and miscarriage after forty

Julie always wanted lots of children, but didn't meet her husband, Ben, until she was in her thirties. They didn't want to try for a family straight away because they wanted to get to know each other properly and enjoy travelling the world. They also wanted to be married when they had children, so Julie didn't try to get pregnant for the first time until she was thirty-three. As a trained nurse and health visitor, she knew there might be fertility issues to face after twenty-seven.

However, Julie wasn't really prepared for the level of difficulty that she actually encountered. 'I was just forty-one when I had my third and last son, Oliver, but I had had so many physical problems before him, that his birth was a real miracle. I had problems conceiving when I first tried to get pregnant. Eventually I got pregnant after six months of trying, and promptly miscarried. It was very traumatic. We both felt devastated as we hadn't really thought it was possible, somehow. Then I got pregnant again, and miscarried again. I got very frightened at this point and saw a gynaecologist who sent me to a fertility clinic. They couldn't find anything wrong, although they said I might have polycystic ovary disease. I had irregular periods, so it was a possibility. It was suggested I take clomid to boost the ovaries and within two months I was pregnant again. My first child, Peter, was eventually born when I was thirty-five. It was an emergency Caesarian after a very long and painful labour, but I was overjoyed and breastfed for a whole year.

'We decided to go ahead and try for another baby. I used clomid and, bingo, fell pregnant again. It was a fairly uneventful pregnancy, but an utterly horrendous delivery. Dean was born just before I was thirty-seven. It was a nightmare and I really thought I was going to die. I was utterly scared for the baby, too, although he was fine, albeit very bruised and battered. What had happened was that they let me go into labour and said I could have a "trial of scar" for eight hours. If you've had a Caesarian before, they do this to see if you can give birth naturally. It was absolute hell. I was progressing only very slowly for twenty hours. Then they said push and I pushed for two hours. They didn't give me pain relief because the epidural failed. Then they said they wanted do a ventouse [suction to remove the baby]. I didn't want an epesiotomy [cut to the perineum, the skin between the vagina and rectum], but I was in excruciating pain. In the end it was a forceps delivery and I remember screaming, "You're hurting me, you're hurting me," and the male doctor saying, "No, I'm not." I said, "It *does* hurt, it's excruciating pain." It felt like someone was pulling my entire insides out. I had a post-partum haemorrhage after the baby was born and I really thought I was dying.

'Dean's birth put me off having another baby. I suffered from post-trauma shock syndrome. I had nightmares and night sweats. I got very tearful if I talked about the birth and I'd get upset if it was mentioned. I felt part of me wasn't all there really, and I worried something was wrong with me, internally. I was incontinent and had to have surgery.

'Eventually, I visited my GP and we chatted about the baby. She then leant forward and said, "But how are *you*?" and I burst into tears. I said, "I'm all right." Then I said, "No, I'm not all right," and burst into floods of tears once more. I told her all about the delivery and she was horrified. She referred me to another consultant and this time I saw a female obstetrician. She went through the whole of the delivery with me in detail - it was very helpful to talk it all through. I think partly it was to make sure no mistakes had been made and, possibly, to put me off taking a case against them. However, I felt afterwards that obstetrics is all about having to make a decision on the spot. There is a degree of judgement that has to be made on the spur of the moment. After all, I'm a health professional and I've been there. I think they didn't make the right judgement and that they should have given me a Caesarian earlier. They should have said "let's get this baby out". Textbook-wise, they probably did make the right decisions, but for me, it was all wrong.

'Anyway, once I'd started being constructive about it all and had been listened to properly by the woman consultant, things began to change. I had surgery and physiotherapy. I had been ripped to shreds and therefore had to be repaired. It didn't completely solve the problem, physically, but they said if I did want any more children (which they advised against), then it would have to be by Caesarian. At that time I didn't want another child, and neither did Ben. I felt I'd had enough and the experience of the last birth had really frightened me off. I thought, "I don't want to go through that again, oh no." However, the post-trauma shock syndrome began to disappear as I dealt with the feelings and the physical problems.

'When Dean got to about two-and-a-half, I began to get broody again. I was thirty-nine then. I told Ben who said, "Oh no, I thought we were done with all that, but I'll think about it." I think he was frightened about what might happen to me because, after all, he'd seen me nearly die and he'd gone through the aftermath with me as well. I left it for a couple of months, but I still felt broody. So I asked Ben again and he said, "Oh well, OK, I agree, but you need to talk to the docs first about the risks. I don't want to lose you." So I went to my new GP thinking, "I'll be forty when I have the next baby." The GP said I was healthy and I could have a Caesarian. He was straight with me about the risks for the baby and for me. He made me think about how I would feel if I were to have a Down's baby. He was very good, I felt.

'After some thought, we decided to go for it. I took clomid again and wham, got pregnant straight away. I thought this was marvellous and then, at about eight weeks, I miscarried. I was utterly devastated. I hadn't realised the baby had died at five weeks because I still felt extremely pregnant. I had to have a d. and c. and it was very upsetting. I thought, "My God I'm forty and miscarrying. That's it for having another baby.' But I still wanted to try again, took clomid, and was pregnant within a couple of months. Then started a roller-coaster of investigations. I thought hard about the tests, talked it through with Ben and the doctors, had a nuchal folds scan at twelve weeks (which was OK), and then had an early amniocentesis at twelve and a half weeks.

'However, the amnio went wrong. Two days before the results were due, the hospital phoned up and said the test had failed to develop and was inconclusive. I was devastated, because I was fifteen weeks pregnant by then and about to go on holiday. They said I could go back in a week to have another test and I said, "No, I want the test tomorrow. I'll be sixteen and a half weeks by next week and that means waiting until I'm nineteen or twenty weeks for a result. That's too late'. They agreed and I had the test the next day. This time, they decided to do a CVS [in which a small sample of placenta is removed through a needle inserted into the uterus via the mother's abdominal wall] instead of an amnio. I do think being older and wiser meant I was more assertive at this point. I was then about to go to Spain and the results hadn't come through. I kept phoning, desperate to know, and eventually got through on ship-to-shore telephone from the Bay of Biscay. I was shouting, "Please can I have the result", above the wind and noise of the engines. Thankfully, everything was fine, and we were able to relax into our holiday.

'On my return, I had a scan at twenty weeks and they said I had a big amniotic sac. I said, "Look I've had big baby boys and I've been very big every time." But the hospital was worried, so they did some investigations. They thought it could be toxoplasmosis. I was thinking, "Whatever will it be next?" The test for that came back negative at twenty-two weeks, but they still wanted to keep an eye on me. I thought it was fine really, because I'd had big babies before. Then the baby became what is called an "unstable lie": first he was breech, then transverse, then head down, then transverse again. I also had a low placenta - called placenta previa - which can be a risk at birth. The baby was tossing around all over the place, even at thirty-four weeks, and it was like having a footballer inside.

'At thirty-five weeks, just before Christmas, the registrar said "I think we'll bring you in for Christmas and deliver you afterwards." But I said, "You can't do that, I've got two small kids at home, you just can't." He explained the waters might break and if I went into labour the blood supply could be cut off due to my low placenta. I replied, "Yes, I see, but all my babies have been late, not early." I really do think my age and experience had something to do with me being able to argue back. I felt able to assess the risks and argue the score. Of course, I had to listen to what he said, but I felt sure it would be OK.

'Physically, I felt very tired at the time. It was harder carrying a baby in my forties than in my thirties. My joints ached, my back, hips and pelvis hurt more, I felt more tired than I had previously (though of course, I was looking after two small kids of three and five as well). But I really wanted to be home with my family over Christmas. When I spoke to my female consultant - who had four children of her own - she was great. She said, "You can go home, but you must come in if there's any sign of any twingeing, OK? You have to get here immediately, no matter what's going on." "Yes," I said, "I do know I'm taking a risk. Thanks." Christmas was fine, and Oliver was born two days afterwards, by Caesarian. It was absolutely fab. It was a crisp snowy day with blue skies coming up over the hills. I said goodbye to the boys, it was a terribly emotional moment, but I was excited. I worried about them, because you are always worried about what you are inflicting on your children and risking having a third at forty-one was an unknown quantity. However, this time I had a spinal anaesthetic which worked perfectly and the delivery was great. The only problem was that I did have a reaction to the spinal afterwards (it's a 1 in 200 chance) and I had the worst headache of my life for three days. This was because spinal fluid was still leaking from where the needle had gone in. However, they took me to surgery and did a "spinal patch" which means they take blood from your arm and immediately inject it into the site of the anaesthetic and it seals up the hole, so you don't leak any more fluid. It worked well and the headache disappeared as I left the theatre.

'I breastfed Oliver (I breastfed all my children for a year each), but I still wanted more children. This time my age stopped me. And Ben really didn't want me to have any more. I thought, "I've had three miscarriages, two Caesarians, a vaginal repair, I've got dodgy joints and a bad back - I ought to call it a day." But still I longed for another. If I had started having my children five years earlier, then I would have gone for a fourth, without doubt. Emotionally, I wanted more, but Ben didn't, and I had to respect his wishes. Age was definitely the deciding factor in my eventually deciding to be sterilised at forty-five.

'As a teenager, I can remember feeling really sorry for kids whose parents looked really old at school open days. I guess I felt I didn't want to put my boys through that later on although, having said that, looking around my local playground, I'm not that unusual. I'd say about two-thirds of the mothers are in their late thirties to mid forties. But I am aware that with my youngest, I'll be fifty-five when he's fifteen and his mates will have mothers who will be twenty years younger than me. But there's not a lot I can do about that, except to keep myself as fit and well as I can. Luckily, I trained as a dancer in my youth, so I'm quite aware of physical fitness and health: I still enjoy walking, swimming and dancing. I look at my three - especially Oliver - and think I'm very, very lucky. I think you're much more patient when you are older (as long as you're not too tired), and wiser. I'm so glad we risked it all again because our family is how complete. I feel I was lucky that medical practice had moved on and I was also old enough to negotiate what I wanted. I think you have to take charge and go for it in life. Certainly, you have to assess the odds and give it a go - I'm just so very glad that we took the risk.'

3

Myth 2: Granny at the School Gate

REALITY TODAY: LATE PARENTS MAKE GREAT PARENTS

Why leave it so late?

'I had my children either side of my fortieth birthday so there are only twenty-one months between them. My daughter is now thirteen-and-a-half, and my son is approaching his twelfth birthday. My husband is eight years younger than me. Both children were very wanted children: I had had a very long life as a singleton and had done all those things I wanted to. I stopped working and was at home for seven years until my son started school. I don't expect we'll ever recover financially, but none of us would regret that decision. I've been working part-time for seven years now, but family comes first. I'm aware that there are not so many years before the children will be independent, so we try to do our best with family holidays, parties and fun... I'm now approaching my fifty-third birthday, which seems a completely bizarre thought, so I suppose they keep me young.'

Penny, writing to me at Home & Life magazine

The above e-mail encapsulates the attitude and experience of so many women who have had their babies late in life.

A long, single, working life, a late marriage to a younger man and then joy and devotion to a much wanted child or children. It sounds a bit like a fairytale, but it is, indeed, the reality for a significant minority today as women having babies over forty constitute 2 per cent of the live birth rate. The numbers will climb as the century continues. While interviewing women for this book, several themes kept emerging as each woman told her story as to why she had left it so late. First, there were *physical* reasons, such as disability, injury, failed pregnancies (abortions, miscarriages, stillbirths or disastrous aftermaths of earlier births or pregnancies), infertility or serious conditions such as multiple sclerosis or cancer (see Myth 4 for more on this) - which had been a bar to pregnancy earlier in life. As medical knowledge and practice has improved and technology advanced, their seemingly insoluble physical problems are now often soluble (see Myth 1 for more on this). This is not true for every woman and of course infertility - for whatever reason - can be an agony which has to be faced and accepted by some. However, there is a greater chance than ever before that physical difficulties which were seen as barriers to birth, even as little as twenty years ago, have been largely conquered (or at least diminished) for many older women today.

Second, there were *circumstantial* reasons, such as being a career woman, being single, not finding the right man, being married to the wrong man or simply 'not being ready' psychologically. Sometimes, Mr Right came after one, two, even three divorces or separations and having a baby was a seal on the relationship. Or, late motherhood came after years of celibacy, or uncommitted relationships, even lesbianism or bisexuality.

These women's mothers would probably have stayed with the same man, whether they were happy or not, out of a sense of duty and obligation. In the bad old days, you made your bed - literally - and you had to lie in it for life (or 'until death us do part'). Contraception was minimal, divorce was difficult, so women put up with loveless or tedious marriages, even abuse, rather than be 'shamed' through separation and divorce. However, for women forty plus, the chance of ending dead-end relationships and moving on to new ones has been possible from the 1960s onwards. Not only was divorce legalised in 1967, but cohabitation became gradually less stigmatised. Serial monogamy and living together is the norm today. Avoiding marriage was controversial in the 1970s, now we hardly notice if people are simply living together or are legally hitched. Back then, it was highly controversial to flout convention, whereas today, agony aunts and counsellors, even parents and religious leaders, actually advise living together before you tie the knot permanently.

More choice, more power

Today, women have become more powerful and discerning about relationships, and more concerned about their emotional and physical welfare. This means women are more picky overall about who to spend their lives with. Some women said to me, candidly, 'Oh, I couldn't have a baby with this man or that man because he simply wasn't the right one.' Others said, 'I simply wasn't ready, I wasn't grown up enough to have a child in my twenties.' Our mothers would probably have settled for less because, after all, they went directly from their fathers' to their husbands' houses, and had little power or choice. There was no concept of 'being ready' back then, you did what was expected. Women's own expectations about what their lives should be about were necessarily lower.

Of course, a good relationship is one that will grow and develop as each partner grows and develops. But some women today feel that men simply do not embrace the challenge to change and therefore the women will grow past their men by mid-life. If a relationship has got 'stuck in a rut' it is very hard to unstick it, unless both partners are willing to be open, admit to problems, and put in the hard work to change not only the shape of the relationship, but also themselves. If a couple have been childless until midlife - for whatever reason - and the woman begins to want to have a child before it is too late, this can put a strain on the relationship. Particularly if the man feels he can't or won't change. Watersheds such as reaching thirty, then forty, really do focus the mind and many women I interviewed said the onset of mid-life made them think again about their relationships and, of course, motherhood.

Melanie Griffith Finds Mr Right - Antonio Banderas - Mid-Life

Melanie Griffith, the Hollywood actress, had four previous marriages (including two marriages to Don Johnson) and a major battle with addiction (alcohol, painkillers). She had two children from her earlier marriages, Alexander, fifteen and Dakota, ten. Finally, she found true love with fellow actor Antonio Banderas. They had a daughter, Stella, now four, when Melanie Griffith was forty-three. They had the baby in Spain: 'Which was really great. I was laughing when I gave birth this time. It was my third time, and Antonio was so sweet. I'd say, "OK, I'm gonna push now", and he'd be hyperventilating and saying: "OK, baby, get in there and push!"' She is currently having fertility treatment because 'I'm dying to have more kids. I'm just not getting pregnant so I hope I'm not too old. But we keep practising.'

Hello! magazine, September 2000

Mid-life crisis

Many women I interviewed said they'd been so focused on their career and on enjoying life to the full, that finding the right man simply passed them by - until forty loomed into view. They'd woken up one morning, still feeling like a twenty-year-old but, seeing a forty-year-old in the mirror, thinking, 'Where did the time go?' or 'What shall I do with the rest of my life?' With middle age and menopause on the horizon, these women did some serious mid-life thinking. In some cases, a way of staving off inevitable middle and old age was to find a man to have a baby with (or to go it alone - see Myth 5). After all, having a baby keeps you young, puts you in touch with younger people and can, to some extent, delay the onset of menopause due to all the oestrogen pumping around your body during pregnancy. For many, like Linda below, having a baby has been the product of facing a mid-life crisis as well as finding Mr Right at long last.

Linda's story: mid-life crisis and finding Mr Right

Linda wrote to my agony column on *Home & Life* magazine in response to my request for women's stories. 'I am forty-three years old and about to have my own baby any time,' she wrote. 'After just about giving up on having a baby, I am very excited. I didn't have an amniocentesis test because of the risk of miscarriage, so fingers crossed that everything goes well and my baby is healthy.'

I followed up her letter, by which time Felicity was a bouncing four-month-old baby. Linda told me her story:

'I know now that I left my husband, Stuart, because of a mid-life crisis. It was one of the hardest decisions I've ever made, but I realised it was just not going to work long-term. So when I reached forty we split up. He was a vet and we'd been married for eleven years. I was a vet dispensary worker, so we worked closely together. I have to say that he didn't really treat me very well, but I put up with it for a long, long time. Having our own business was a real pressure, and he took all his bad feelings out on me. I think I'd been brought up to shoulder responsibility and take it on the chin. But by the time I got to forty I began to think, "Where am I going in my life?" and "What am I doing with this man, who treats me like this?" I could see the future stretching ahead and it looked very bleak, I can tell you. I realised, painfully, he wasn't my Mr Right at all.

'I'd wanted children earlier in our marriage and each time I asked him "Shall we try for a baby?" Stuart would come up with some reason as to why it was the wrong time. It was the lambing season, so I couldn't get pregnant (risk of toxoplasmosis), or it was the end of the tax year (pressure to do accounts). I couldn't do anything right for him, he criticised and belittled me all the time, and our marriage was really going nowhere. I realised you could still love somebody, but not like them for a lot of the time.

'When I turned forty, which seemed hugely significant, I left my husband. I packed up and went to stay with an old friend in another city. Martin was a pharmacist and he needed a dispenser who could go round all the old folks' homes. He was very kind to me. He helped me out financially and the best thing was he listened. He was five years younger than me, but he was mature and thoughtful. We had a lot in common, such as fell walking and climbing, so we'd go off in groups and have good weekends out in the fresh air. I'd always liked him, but not in *that* sort of way. He liked me, too, and I trusted him. Martin knew my husband had treated me badly and he kept saying I didn't deserve it and that was very helpful in the first few weeks while I was filing for divorce. The best part was that he made me laugh - he always could - and we'd spend hours talking and laughing; it was really great.

'Not long - probably a couple of months - after I'd moved cities, we became lovers. He was a friend-turned-lover, I suppose, and we started living together properly. We really fell in love and it was wonderful. My husband became insanely jealous - he assumed the worst even when it was still a platonic friendship - and he was ringing up night and day, shouting and harassing down the phone.

'I was terribly upset about the whole situation with Stuart. Even though we were divorcing, I hadn't made him sell the house or anything. I just wanted out of the whole situation. And then I got pregnant. I was utterly amazed - I'd never been pregnant in my life - although, of course, we were having lots of sex. I'm very fit, but I was over forty and I suppose I thought it wouldn't happen because it never had. I haven't got a clue why I got pregnant, except that we left off contraception, thinking it wouldn't happen.

'The doctor couldn't believe it either. I went to him at seven weeks and said, "I'm pregnant" and he said, "How old are you?" When I told him, he looked very surprised. However, the pregnancy was great, I think because I'm very fit and active. I'd take the dogs for long walks and still went fell walking and climbing, plus working long hours. I'm like that - happy when busy. I didn't have any of the tests done because I thought this is my one chance, and I didn't want to risk a miscarriage having an amniocentesis. If it had been a Down's baby, there's no way I could have got rid of it, so it didn't really matter whether we knew or not. Even so, I worried all the time as to whether or not it was all right.

'Martin was thrilled, but also a bit daunted by fatherhood. He said "I'm no good with children", but in fact he's been a devoted father, he's absolutely wonderful. We went to an NCT class, but I was the oldest there, so I felt a bit odd. When I said I was forty-three, one woman exclaimed "Crikey, you don't look that old." The class was useful, but I would have liked to have met other, older mothers. I now have one friend who had a baby at forty-three last year (she didn't intend to have any more), and it's been very helpful to compare notes. After the NCT class, however, I didn't actually follow the birth plan or anything, I just went with the flow, whatever happened. In fact, I ended up being induced because labour lasted nearly thirty hours and they said the baby was in distress. I'm only size 8, so I think it was a tight fit. However, after thirty-eight weeks, I had a wonderful, healthy baby girl. My mother, who is sixty-four, was virtually doing cartwheels down the street, she was so happy.

'The best thing about being an older mother is that I'm very patient with the baby. I'm patient with animals and discovered I love babies because really they're just animals, too. Although I'm over forty, my body recovered very quickly. The physiotherapist gave me exercises and I'm back to size 8-10. I couldn't breastfeed - the milk just didn't come - so I bottle fed her. But I did it in a way that was similar to breastfeeding - very quiet and snuggly, a special time for her and me together, and we bonded strongly. In fact, I've decided to stay home now until she's five. I would like another baby, but I think it would be chancy. If I was younger, I'd go for it straight away. But I think I've been so lucky, I should really enjoy this one while she is young. My mother's an only child and if Felicity turns out anything like her, she won't go far wrong. I've got other friends with only children and they're perfectly all right, too.

'I have very high energy levels - I think I'm just one of those people. I'm vegetarian, don't smoke and only have a couple of glasses of white wine occasionally. I wouldn't get drunk having a baby, it would be too irresponsible. I haven't come across anyone yet saying I'll be a granny at the school gate. I think you're as old as you feel, it's an attitude of mind. I'm just not one of those people who sits on her backside all day and I intend to keep myself as fit as I can through walking, horse riding, whatever. And I'm going to take Felicity too, I'm determined to. The dogs (cocker spaniel and Cavalier spaniel) have been fine with her. I think they were my babies before Felicity came along, but they've really adjusted well. When I look back, I really feel so incredibly lucky. Had I stayed with Stuart life would have continued bleak, dull, dreadful and, of course, I never would have had my daughter. I'm so glad I took the risk and left and so glad that Martin turned out to be Mr Right after all. It's a happy ending or rather, in my case, a happy beginning. Mid-life doesn't seem half so daunting now as it did, I can tell you.'

Finding a younger Mr Right

Finding a younger Mr Right was a recurrent theme among the women I interviewed. One of the knock-on effects of women looking and acting younger (as we saw in Myth 1, forty being the new thirty), is that they may well attract men who are substantially younger than themselves.

Madonna's Search for the Right Younger Mr Right

Madonna, the Queen of Pop, was thirty-eight when she fell pregnant with her first child, Lourdes. The father was her personal trainer, Carlos Leon. 'I can totally relate to the whole idea of getting to a certain age and not feeling like I had met my soulmate, and being in a state of panic about having a child.' Although the relationship ended, she has maintained a friendship with Carlos and he remains a regular carer for Lourdes. Then British Film Director Guy Ritchie, who is ten years younger than Madonna, came on the scene and at forty-one, Madonna had her second child, Rocco, with him. 'He makes me laugh. I love the English sense of humour, it's dry and ironic. English boys are so sexy.' They married in a well publicised, but highly secretive five-day event in Skibo Castle, Scotland, in December 2000. Madonna, now forty-two, has a proper father for her children. 'I think the role of the father in general is as important as the mother's,' she says. 'If you have the luxury of both, you're a very lucky person.'

Quotes taken from *Now* magazine, May 2000

Sadly, the relationship with Guy Ritchie ended, although he remains a devoted father.

Just why younger men are attracted to older women is a subject for discussion in itself, and for which there is not much space here. It is too simplistic to say older women are simply mother figures. Many of the younger men actually take the lead when it comes to trying for children. Perhaps it does come down to life experience and personality, in that the younger man may well not feel challenged enough by a younger or same age partner. Or perhaps they have had very positive experiences of older women (siblings, mothers, friends), which has led them to seek out older women. For some, it is simply the fact of falling in love with the *person,* not their age. This was certainly the case for Lennie who fell in love with Andrea. 'It was wonderful to fall in love with a much younger Mr Right after years of marriage to a definite Mr Wrong,' says Andrea.

Andrea's story: finding a younger Mr Right and having a baby over forty

Andrea, a forty-two-year-old secretary, also wrote to me at *Home & Life:* 'I had been married about thirteen years to my previous husband. I didn't want children with him at all, absolutely definite. It was two things really - first, I never really wanted children myself. I didn't have a longing to have a child - at least - not until I met my current partner. Second, I think my husband was constantly depressed, which was dreadful. He had bouts of depression and shut me out for long periods of time. When I met my new partner, Lennie, it was a classic. He came to work on the garden and there was an instant, mutual attraction. I was thirty-eight; he was thirty. We had an affair and we fell in love. I soon knew it was serious and I moved out and set up home with Lennie. My husband had a nervous breakdown and it was a terrible time. But I knew Lennie and I were right for each other and in fact, I'd considered leaving my husband many times over the years. I'd stayed because I was naive and young when I married and thought I should stick it out, regardless.

'Anyway, Lennie wanted kids and I suddenly found myself wanting them, too. I found myself thinking, "Ooh, he'd make a wonderful father" and feeling all broody and emotional. I came off the Pill - I was forty-and-a-half by then - and the doctor told me to come back if nothing happened in eighteen months. I was back within two months, pregnant, and the doctor laughed, "you don't waste any time, do you?"

'Lennie and I were both over the moon and thrilled to bits. The pregnancy was problem-free. I had Phoebe at forty-two weeks. They threatened to induce me and I think the very word "induce" set me off. However, I had a Caesarian as I couldn't push the baby out in the end. She was a little girl, a perfect 7 lb. 5 oz. and I was forty-one. Lennie wants us to marry now we have a child, but I'm resisting. It could be because of my last marriage ending in disaster. If I regret anything, it's that I didn't meet Lennie earlier so we could have had a crack at having two kids together. Phoebe's such a fantastic little girl and something so special, that I never realised until I had her how deep the feeling goes. The age difference is really no problem. Most people don't realise how old I am! I go horse riding, walking, to the gym. We're just so happy together - and I'm happy to be a mum - I'm glad I had a chance to have a child with Lennie before popping my clogs. I can't imagine my life without her now.'

Changing life choices

Linda's and Andrea's stories are both heartwarming because they have such positive endings. They both were obviously very lucky, but they each also took a tough decision to leave an abusive or loveless marriage which paid off. They took a risk. Of course, there are many women who have simply not found Mr Right (younger, same age or older), or who have only realised, post-menopause in their fifties or sixties, that they really longed for a child all along. Maybe they stayed with the wrong man because they felt they ought to or had no real choice to leave. Some women will be happily single, some will be sad. Many married mothers will envy their single counterparts their freedom; while many single childless women may yearn for a measure of domestic chaos.

Of course, we all make life choices. But what informs those life choices has changed out of all recognition over the past forty years. Women who now are in their forties were in their teens and twenties during the 1960s and 1970s. This was a time of incredible social upheaval. Women burned their bras and threw off the chains of convention concerning sex, marriage and motherhood. Domestic drudgery was out, women's liberation was in. It was an exciting era and with the availability of the Pill, women were able to explore their sexuality and relationships in a completely new way. By the mid-1970s legislation came in giving women new legal rights. The Equal Pay Act (1970) and Sex Discrimination Act (1976) enshrined women's right to participate in the workforce, in education and training, for equal pay. This meant women had new choices. No longer was their path determined by biology and culture: they could choose a variety of paths. And many women chose to put their jobs, careers and money-earning or other life-enhancing activities before motherhood.

Emotional literacy

At the same time, women were learning to be emotionally literate. This meant, through women's groups, better education, therapy and counselling, that they were able to articulate better than ever what they wanted in life. No longer happy to be motherly doormats like many of their own mothers may have been, these women wanted to have opportunities and experiences on an equal basis to men. They wanted to be taken seriously. They wanted to live. This kind of rejection of tradition filtered through to popular culture and newspapers, magazines, TV and radio which imbibed the language of feminism and turned it into everyday parlance. Today, we have absorbed most of these radical, path-breaking notions and it is simply accepted that women will be sexually free and in control of their fertility, able to earn their own money, go to work and choose not only if, but when, whether, how and with whom they will have babies.

Back in the 1970s and 1980s new Maternity Rights legislation again made it possible for women to have children and keep their jobs. Although fairly minimalist, it did at least put down a marker which said - 'Even if I have a baby, I'll want to continue to be independent through being able to continue working, even if only part-time.' Hence, women who are having their babies in their forties today will have lived through an important era - whether they were themselves radically involved or not - which put women's rights, independence, education and equality at work first. They may well have sacrificed love relationships, opportunities to marry and having children for the sake of their independence and self-respect. Back in the 1970s it seemed like it was either/ or. Either you lived the kind of life your mother lived before you, or you struck out, rejected convention, and lived a life never lived before. Of course, many women did follow the traditional path, but they were nonetheless influenced by the Zeitgeist, the spirit of the times.

Having it all

But why, having rejected motherhood at the usual time (twenties and thirties), have some women gone on to have a baby forty plus? Many I spoke to came to the conclusion that in the end career, financial independence and sexual freedom *were not enough*. By going all out for liberty they found they had in fact denied themselves some very basic human pleasures and rights. Even the icon of feminism and author of the groundbreaking *Female Eunuch,* Germaine Greer, realised - albeit too late - that she had changed from not wanting babies, to desperately wanting them.

The truth is, many women, like Germaine Greer above, moved beyond the initial need to reject everything traditional to the point where they could hold on to the bits which were good, fulfilling and valuable while trying to integrate them into a more complicated, late twentieth-century lifestyle. Of course, women are still struggling with how to 'have it all' today. Articles on 'When is the right time to have a baby?' or 'Should I put career or baby first?' abound in women's magazines. More choice has brought with it more complexity. Accompanying greater freedom is a greater anxiety about 'getting it right'. The twenty-first century is more of an era of seeking perfection - women want it all, right now (i.e. have a baby with Mr Right, be successful, rich and beautiful *and* stay slim), which is usually impossible. This means, as the century continues, the vexed question of if, how, where, when, with whom to have a baby will be an increasingly complex one to answer. Each woman will clearly have to answer it for herself as there are no blanket solutions.

Germaine Greer's Change of Heart

'All I knew about babies when I was growing up was that they were seriously bad news. Getting pregnant meant the end of all good times, morning sickness, bloating, loss of looks; producing a child meant not a triumph and rejoicing, but the banishment of sleep, baby-sick down your neck, a constant tide of baby urine and faeces, and baby washing forever steaming up the windows. The mother-generation warned us darkly not to rush into child-bearing, to have a "good time" while we could.' Then Germaine housed one of her pregnant students and fell in love with her new baby. 'I fully expected that when the baby came home, the quality of life would take a nosedive. In fact, baby Ruby screamed from eight-o'clock until midnight every night of the first three months of her life. Strangely, I didn't mind. I walked her and soothed her and flattened the colic bubbles by laying her on my chest. I drove her in the car until she fell asleep... I found her scrumptious, delicious, ineffable, adorable, and was astonished. If anyone had told me that the happiest experiences of my life would include falling asleep on my big bed with Ruby's baby-hand sleepily stroking my cheek, or feeling her fall asleep as I intoned the fable of the most beautiful frog in the world, or dancing round a car park with her on my hip, I would have been incredulous.'

Aura magazine, June 2000

Change of direction

The ability to change direction mid-life is quite an art and I found many of the women I interviewed were not only able, but more than willing, to do this. A change of direction will obviously bring about some very fundamental and important life changes. One of the most extraordinary stories I discovered was a woman who was a nun for over ten years earlier in her life, and who is now a mother forty plus. Back then, not only were marriage and babies out of the question for her, but also men and sexual relationships. Yet, at forty-six she was utterly surprised to find herself pregnant (although she knew it wasn't an immaculate conception).

Patience's story: a total change of direction at forty

Patience is no longer a 'Sister'. She is now a 56-year-old mother, of a boisterous and challenging ten-year-old daughter, Helena, living in relative rural isolation in an Oxfordshire rectory with her husband, the vicar.

'I wasn't planning to have kids - ever,' she says candidly, 'it was a total mistake, it just happened, really. I think it came as such a surprise because it wasn't what I had expected to do with my life. I was in a convent for about ten years from 1973 to 1983. I was twenty-nine when I came out. I had been very happy there for ten years, but it became clear to me that I would not be there for the rest of my life. I first of all worked in publishing, which was a real eye-opener. Then I gravitated towards working with people with mental problems. I felt that was more "real", more me. I worked in homes for the elderly and I met my husband through work. I don't really make decisions about things, I tend to drift. I don't think about the future or plan, either, so I sort of drifted into getting married. I'd managed not to get married for so long, that it was a bit of a shock. But my new life was a complete change and it sort of made sense. With hindsight, I'm not quite sure why I did it really, but oddly it has been quite a successful marriage.

'I found him fun, I suppose, and we shared common goals. He was a good friend, too. I suppose we fell in love. At odd moments I definitely remember feeling in love with him, whatever that means. Anyway, we wanted to live together, but we couldn't really, as he was the vicar. It wouldn't have looked too good, would it? So we married. In fact, I think we married because he's one of the few people I've met it's been possible to live with.

'We weren't thinking about children. After all, we weren't twenty, so we didn't take any of it seriously. Anyway, he had two children in their thirties from his first marriage, so we settled into a sort of working companionship. I didn't know much about sex, of course, I hadn't got a clue. So I went and bought a cap, read the instructions, and stuck it in every time we had sex. I think I did it right, although perhaps subconsciously I stopped being so conscientious about it. But it was never on my agenda to have a baby. I'd never had a strong drive to have children because I always had other things I wanted to do with my life. It was an incredible mistake. I remember I was sitting reading a novel around Easter time. My breasts felt tender and I thought: My breasts really are sore. Surely I can't be pregnant, no that's silly. I couldn't possibly be. I went to Boots and got a kit, pretending it was for somebody else. I did a test and it was positive. I couldn't believe it, so I did another one. It was positive again. I thought it must be a mistake, so I went to the doctor and he thought it was a mistake, too, so he did a test. It was positive. *I really was pregnant.* I went in to work (I was working for a mental health charity at the time - working in night shelters voluntarily and living on benefits) and everyone roared with laughter when I told them. It was clearly some sort of cosmic joke, not part of my scene at all. Everyone thought it was really funny. I was actually four months pregnant by then. We'd just moved house, I was really busy at work and vaguely thought I was having an early menopause when my periods stopped. I'm quite detached from my body, really, so I don't notice these things much.

'I'm not very maternal, but I looked around and thought: Well, a lot of other people have babies and they can do it OK. So I thought I could manage it. The doctor said I had a 1 in 18 chance of the baby having Down's syndrome, so I had an amniocentesis. I don't know if I would have had an abortion if the baby had been Down's, but I wanted to know. All was fine. I didn't go to antenatal classes, and the pregnancy was fine. Although I'm overweight, I'm very fit and I wasn't at all ill. The birth was relatively straightforward, although I had to have a Caesarian. Even though a foot came out they decided it was easier for me to be unzipped and have her taken out. I couldn't breastfeed her, however, even though I saw the world's greatest breastfeeding expert. I couldn't get the hang of it at all. I didn't enjoy that bit. I felt pressurised by the "we must breastfeed" thing. In the end, I looked at this feeble, crying pathetic thing and said, "I can't breastfeed this child, give her a bottle."

'With hindsight, I can see I had absolutely no idea what I was doing. When I came home from hospital I laid a lovely stone floor. It's a bit uneven, but it's good. However, I think I possibly should have got some more rest instead. Maybe breastfeeding would have gone better, I don't know. Anyway, life went on and I went back to work part-time when Helena was fifteen months. I found a childminder who was delightful and who taught me a lot, I said to her one day, "Susie, isn't it about time Helena got some teeth?" and she said, "Look, she's got loads of teeth at the back." I'm not very good at all those physical things. But she is a fit little thing in that she's only been to the doctor three times since she was born. It might be that I haven't noticed how ill she is, or maybe she's really healthy. Anyway, she was sleeping really well after six weeks and I was getting twelve hours sleep a night. I thought well, that's not too bad, although I couldn't bring myself to say this to other, younger, mothers who were clearly suffering from lack of sleep. But I wasn't very clued up about doing all the bit about checking she was breathing. I wasn't worried about her in that way at all.

'I never had another period after Helena was born. I had an early menopause and one hot flush on my fiftieth birthday. I didn't notice it really, it was just a relief not to have periods any more. As a mother, I didn't really understand how much I'd have to do at first. And my husband hasn't been the most involved of fathers, even though he was very excited about the baby when I was pregnant. I do get pissed off that he doesn't do more. I think he had a difficult divorce and he has focused on having good relationships with his own older kids. But for the first five or six years he was really pathetic with Helena, leaving it all to me. I was very cross and resentful a lot of the time, although once I stopped being so cross, I could understand it more. I've learned to do swaps with other mothers, so Helena has friends to play with. I've also made an effort for her to meet her cousins, although they are all substantially older than her. I think she misses having brothers and sisters and being a single child is an issue for her. She also doesn't have any grandparents living and that is a regret.

'But, as for my mothering skills, I've had to learn on the job. I'm quite laid back and not very good at keeping up discipline, rules and boundaries - those sorts of things. I can be very nice and quiet and then suddenly crack and start yelling at her to "for God's sake, shut up" or something. My mum died when Helena was about three (she didn't really know her) and I had a little box of jewellery that I associate with her. I found Helena wearing the contents and I was absolutely furious, pushed her on the sofa and walked out. Sometimes, I feel I might hit her, but I always walk away. I don't feel proud of that and we make up afterwards. I don't think I talk down to her, I talk to her as an adult. But I do love her a lot and she knows it. She now goes to the tiny village school and I'm back at work full-time.

'We have family holidays, and I stay in and read and my husband goes out on long walks, Helena usually stays with me. She's not that bright, but she's into Barbie and the Spice Girls, the usual package. I think I'm quite up on all that now, plus social issues, which obviously I learn about at work. Helena has never asked me why I'm so old. She takes me for the scruffy old mum that I am - at least, she says she loves me as I am. I don't feel bad about my age. I think well, that's life. Tough. That's who you've got. Tough things happen and you have to learn to live with them. I think, overall, that I am very happy to have had a child. Looking back, I never would have wanted one earlier, I couldn't have coped with it. I think I'm more patient and relaxed than I would have been when I was younger, more accepting and understanding about what happens. I'm able to take what comes and get on with it. Helena knows some nuns from my old convent and she's never really asked me about my previous life. I think she just takes me for who I am. I think, all in all, it's worked out in the most fortunate way.'

Not 'being ready'

Of course, Patience's story is an extraordinary one. However, it illustrates how none of us can know at the outset of our lives exactly how we will end up. It proves what the old adage advises: never say never. Certainly, many of the women who were interviewed for this book said the reason they had left motherhood so late was because they were simply 'not ready' on an emotional level before their forties. This was certainly true of me. Women used to have children because they were expected to, ready or not. Today, we are a much more 'emotionally literate' culture and women (and men) are conscious that they may not 'be ready' to have children earlier than forty. This can be because it takes time for the emotional damage from childhood to be healed through counselling and therapy; or it may be a matter simply of maturing, or working through problems in other ways - becoming highly creative, travelling the world, living abroad. Some people burn out their pain through sowing wild oats or by being heavily addicted to drink, drugs, spending or sex, before 'recovering' enough to have a normal life. The urge to 'settle down' may only occur once a woman or a man has been able to 'work through' whatever put them off procreating earlier in life. Perhaps it's too late (physically), and sometimes people consciously decide not to have children, because they are unable to make the sacrifices they inevitably involve.

Yet, for some women, 'being ready' and being able to have a child late in life can be the most wonderfully effective way to heal past hurts. This can provide a means of righting the past without repeating it (particularly important for survivors of all kinds of abuse - emotional, physical, sexual). It is likely such women will have been through much more life experience, be more willing to read parenting books and go to parenting classes, and seek out appropriate advice when necessary. They may well be more self-aware, more conscious of and reflective about their foibles and able to admit their mistakes, than younger mothers. An older parent may have had a chance to have some therapy or counselling, which can prepare them for parenthood on a psychological level.

Madonna Healed by Her Child

Wild child Madonna's own mother died when she was five. She says of her youth: 'I shudder to think about some of the things I did ... everyone goes through their youthful rebellion stage - except that I had mine in my thirties.' Madonna says she named her daughter Lourdes (whom she had when she was thirty-eight) after the French village famous for miracle cures and religious healing. 'Every time I look into her eyes, I feel healed.' Being a late mum 'made me realise what I had missed by my mother dying. It makes me feel inspired to give my daughter everything I didn't have.'

Quoted in Now magazine, May 2000

Overprotective or self-aware?

There is a common belief that older parents will stifle their children by being overprotective. Of course, this is a risk, especially if the long-awaited child is an only child. There can be a danger of it becoming a 'chosen child', one that is worshipped and not really allowed to be a child, making mistakes, being silly, fallible, rude - in fact, just plain ordinary (see John Bradshaw's thought-provoking book, *The Chosen Child Syndrome* (Piatkus)). Late parents need to keep things in perspective: it's not possible to do a perfect job and one's child won't be perfect. It is important to keep other interests going, otherwise too much weight and importance can settle on a young child's shoulders. Children need space to be 'ordinary', not performing parrots, filling their parents' needs for them.

Addicted to babies

Another emotional pitfall to watch for is addiction. Some women literally become addicted to babies. This is an emotional addiction - to being 'full' (emotionally and literally), feeling a sense of importance and worth, needing to be depended upon. For some women over forty, who may either be facing the menopause without having had children or the 'empty nest syndrome' when older children have left home, there can be a real pull towards filling the gap with a baby. The recent case, cited in the *Mirror* 27 January 2001, of Sue Povey giving birth to her fourteenth child at forty-one, is typical. She says of her desire to have children: 'I just adore newborn babies. I thought I could give them up, but it's an addiction. I'm a babyholic.'

The problem is, that if babies are had to meet the need of an addiction, then the children themselves usually do not get the attention they need long term. Some women will continue to risk miscarriage or spend all their savings on IVF treatment, rather than face the emptiness they feel inside. Mid-life can seem daunting, and filling it with a baby can seem a tempting way of staving off the inevitable ageing process. Sometimes the desire for a baby will be driven by loss - loss of a parent, or loss of a partner or husband through divorce, separation and death (which makes the woman want to fill the emptiness and heal the rejection). Any woman who feels this could be true of her should seek counselling or therapy *before* leaping into late motherhood. The problem is that babies grow up, and once they become small children they will inevitably need to push their mothers away as psychological separation starts (a healthy process). A mother who has had a baby out of addiction may take pushing away as a personal rejection (which it isn't), and may well begin to feel the desperate longing to fill the gap again. Having babies addictively isn't about having babies, it's about trying to keep an addiction satisfied. And the nature of addiction is to never be satisfied, to always need the next fix - in this case, a baby. (See the section on Further Reading for practical advice in my book *Overcoming Addiction*.)

However, the dangers of either making a baby a 'chosen child' or having it out of an addictive urge, is usually outweighed by the fact that forty-plus mothers will probably be more self-aware and conscious of the pitfalls surrounding late motherhood, due to their own life experience. This was true of Sandra, who is now sixty-five, and who had her only son at forty-five. She wrote to me at *Home & Life:*

Sandra's story: overcoming childhood pain just in time

'My mother was a very bad mother and really put me off motherhood. I think if I'd been a mother in my twenties I would have been a very bad mother, too. I'm sure I would have followed her pattern automatically. She was hell on wheels: incredibly vicious, never consistent, saying "I'm going to kill myself" or "I can't stand you" every five minutes. Looking back, I can see that she was mentally ill, a manic depressive, but as a child, I was frightened of her all the time. Some women are very fortunate in having had mothers who were capable and good to them. I feel bitter sometimes that my mother was so awful, I was an only child myself and I think I decided very early on to avoid motherhood altogether. My father was quite weak and didn't really stand up to her. She was meaner to me than she was to him. Finally, he died when he was sixty-two of a heart attack - he was drawing the curtains at the time. Then she remarried and my step-father also died of a stroke (he phoned me before he died, saying he couldn't stand her any more and was utterly stressed out). Typically, she survived them both, she's a kind of bloodsucker.

'Anyway, I didn't marry until I was thirty-nine. I think I was very frightened of a commitment like marriage, coming from my family. I'd worked all my life as a hospital radiographer, so I think I was a real career woman at heart. I'd had three long, important relationships with men before. The nearest I got to marriage was with an Australian, but he didn't want to marry and settle in England; so we became friends in the end. I met my husband through a mutual friend. He was going out with a girl I shared a flat with, but soon made it clear he was interested in me. However, he was twelve years younger, so I didn't really take him seriously. Although we have similar aspirations and beliefs, we had very different hobbies - he plays golf and skis, which I don't. However, we both like travelling in France and Spain, exploring the open road, hiring a villa, that sort of thing. I'm a lapsed Catholic and he's C of E, so we have very different perspectives on life, but none of it mattered. We fell in love.

'He was at the bottom of his career in chartered surveying and I was at the top (he was twenty-seven, I was thirty-nine) when we married. I earned more than he did, but it wasn't a problem. We decided to buy a house in the country and we sold his flat and my house and bought a huge rectory in the Suffolk countryside. We'd discussed having kids before we married, but I made it clear it was largely impossible. Not only did my family history make it feel undesirable, but I had had TB of the spine as a child and only had one fallopian tube working. At thirty-nine, with this problem, getting pregnant seemed pretty remote. I just thought I would never, ever be a mum.

'We didn't use contraception for five years. I then felt the first hot flush and thought: "Oh Lord, it's the menopause, now I'll never have a baby." It did make me feel very sad. I was forty-five by then. We went to Chartres with friends and I lit a candle in the cathedral and found myself praying, "God, is it too late? I'd really like to have a baby. Please help me." Six weeks later I was pregnant. I didn't realise for a long time that I was, as my periods were a bit awry - I just thought it was the old menopause setting in. I went to stay with a pregnant girlfriend for the weekend, and though I usually have a very healthy appetite, I told her "I can't eat very well at present." I also didn't fancy drinking any wine - which is unlike me. She said, "Do you think you're pregnant?" But I laughed and said, "No way, it must be the menopause or a tummy bug or something." Nonetheless, I bought a pregnancy test the next day and it was positive. I remember my husband was out playing golf at the time and I burst into tears. When he came home I told him and he said, "Does that mean we're going to have a baby?" I said, I thought so, and we were utterly amazed and excited.

'Of course, when I told my mother she was a real grouch about it. All she said was: "I don't suppose it'll be all right." Meaning, I expect it will be deformed or something. She used to be a nurse and she would always look on the black side about everything, especially anything pertaining to me. She had to pour cold water on it and couldn't bear me being happy. But I suppose by then I understood she was like that and although it hurt, it didn't really deter me. Our friends hooted with laughter. Me having a baby at forty-five was an absolute shock to them. But my doctor was wonderful, an absolute rock. He said, "Great, fine, let's get you the best care possible," and sent me to the Royal London Hospital to see a consultant. However, when I saw a young registrar there, his first comment was, "You don't have to go through with this, you know." I said, "Look, I've worked twenty-eight years in hospitals and have seen all sorts of things - I'm having this baby, OK?" Apart from him, all the midwives were utterly wonderful.

'I had no complications during pregnancy and because I'm a radiographer I was not allowed to work [X rays would harm a foetus]. Instead, I was put on sick leave and told to go home and rest for five months. I was told to lie down for a couple of hours every afternoon, and I did until the end.

'I felt fine and had absolutely no problems at all. I had an elective Caesarian at thirty-nine weeks and Alex was born at 8 lb. 4 oz. We were utterly thrilled with the baby. I was as fit as anyone else on the ward. All I'd had were slightly swollen ankles at the end, otherwise I was fine. Of course, my mother refused to come and see the baby. She was being very difficult about it. However, my mother-in-law came to stay and looked after us all. She was both delightful and delighted, and made up for my mother's continuing negativity.

'I wasn't able to breastfeed as I have inverted nipples and I was sad about that, but Alex was perfectly happy on a bottle. I went back to work nine months after he was born, but missed him too much. I had tried a childminder, but she wasn't too bright. So, although my husband was not too far up the ladder in his career, we started to live on one, much smaller, salary. That was hard, but by my age I didn't really care about the latest fashions and trivia like that. We could manage. Of course, after that we wanted another child, but by forty-eight the menopause had really set in. I am sad we didn't have another one, but he has turned out fine, nonetheless. Alex is now nineteen and I think he's a very intelligent, confident boy - I should say man - he has left home now and is at university doing Hispanic studies. He's much more grown up than I was at his age. He went to Ecuador during his gap year and travelled round, keeping in touch with us by e-mail and phone. Of course, I worried about him, but I would never try to hold him back. I'm not overprotective – or at least, I try not to be. He did smoke for a while, but gave it up. He does drink quite a lot, but this generation does - especially the girls, it seems. He does talk to me about his loves and life and we're pretty close. We go to the local pub together for a pint and some lunch, and have a long talk about everything, just like old friends. He also plays cricket and football with my husband, although I'm not so good at that physical stuff due to my hips being bad now.

'As for my mother, we had a period of estrangement when I was fifty. She came for Christmas and was so atrocious I said to my husband afterwards, "I'm not having this any more." We didn't speak for two years, although my husband used to take my son over for visits. Eventually, she went into sheltered accommodation near us and we guardedly got back in touch. She died of salmonella poisoning which she caught on a hospital visit six years ago. We did get on better as she got older - perhaps because she saw me being a mother at last and it healed something for us both. I think the fact that I hadn't had children was a signal to her that she had been a bad mother - which was true - but she blamed me for it. Being a mother - albeit a late mother - also made me understand how hard the job was for her. I think she began to respect and like me, especially when I X-rayed her inmate friends who said, "Oh your daughter's so nice." She stopped thinking, then, that I was the worst daughter in the world.'

Late parents make great parents

The stereotype of forty-plus parents being boring old fogies who are emotionally illiterate and out of touch with the modern world is simply untrue today. One forty-five-year-old mother interviewed for this book told me that she had taken her child round the world at two and that he'd regularly gone skiing and snowboarding with her and accompanied her on diving expeditions. At four, he could already do the crawl and was used to climbing on and off planes. Of course, it's down to the individuals concerned and their own particular circumstances, but the notion that older parents will simply hand over their offspring to a nanny and go back to work, or that they will be boring and unable to play sport, or not be interested in living life to the full, is simply outdated and inaccurate. There are plenty of unadventurous young fogies in their twenties or thirties with rigid attitudes or fixed ideas - it's *who* you are, *not* how old you are, that really counts.

Mother and grandmother rolled into one

The pioneering research undertaken by Julia Berryman, lately of Leicester University's Parenthood Research Group, shows unequivocally that: 'Mothers are good mothers over forty. Their attitudes towards child-rearing are very different from younger mothers. They are more patient, have a higher opinion of themselves, are generally more relaxed and invest more in motherhood. Because they have done a lot of things in life before motherhood they can focus on their children without feeling they are missing out.' Interestingly, older fathers also seem to have a more egalitarian approach to their children, treating boys and girls more similarly than younger fathers might. There is also a wider issue, which is that forty plus mothers are probably more settled and/or happier in their relationship. They usually have more money and time to spend on and with the child. 'The result', according to Julia Berryman, 'is that the children of older parents tend to be brighter, have better reading scores and higher self-esteem.' This is usually because an older mother will make the space to nurture and teach, rather like a grandmother and mother rolled into one. This is certainly true of some high-flying women who have decided to take the plunge into late motherhood and make it a success, just like their earlier careers have been.

Yvonne's story: giving up work to have a child at forty-four

Yvonne was running her own PR company when, at forty-two, she finally married her childhood sweetheart.

'Because we'd known each other since being teenagers, we giggled when the vicar said he'd say a prayer for us having children. I mean, it was ridiculous, we were in our forties. I have to say that all my life I'd wanted bundles of children - at least five - so it was a lingering hope. But we didn't really think it would work out and at that time we had no regrets. I'd had a wonderful career, working abroad and making money, so I didn't think I really minded not having children. However, my husband did want a child and it was an issue that wouldn't really go away. We stopped using contraception - just in case - and were utterly over the moon when I got pregnant in the spring of 1995. It was the first time in my life, and I was forty-three and very excited. We had been living apart for some time, with me working in London, and him working in Eastern Europe. However, he came back to London and I had a miscarriage at seven weeks. I was utterly shattered as I hadn't expected either to be pregnant in the first place, or then to lose the baby.

'My GP was extremely helpful and understanding, telling me that it doesn't always work out first time, but do not give up. I said, "Hell, look at my age, I'm lucky to have got pregnant at all." He was very kind to me, coming out in the night and giving me a lot of time and attention. I fell pregnant a couple of months later and thought, "Wow, this might really happen this time", only to miscarry seven weeks later.

'Panic began to set in. I think I'd been in self-denial up until this point, thinking "I'm forty-three, it's too late, it won't happen." So when it did, twice, it whetted my appetite. Because I *could* get pregnant, I suddenly wanted a child very, very much. I couldn't deny it to myself any longer and suddenly it became the number one priority in my life. My husband, John, was back in England for good by then and I presented him with a monumental decision I had come to while he was away working: I wanted to leave work in order to have a child. I earned extremely well at this time, and I was at the top of my career, at Managing Director level. If I had continued, who knows where I might have ended up? Heading up a major international company on a vast salary? But all I knew at this time was I wanted a baby very badly - badly enough to give up everything for it.

'We decided to move out to Oxfordshire to live a quieter, more healthy lifestyle and we found a nice place to buy. At first, I was fully prepared to drive up and down the M4 or hop on a train to London for meetings, but I felt very stressed out at the thought. I was so worried about my two pregnancies not lasting that I thought: Why not sweep everything clean? My job demanded a commitment of seven days a week, twenty-four hours a day, and I knew if I wanted a baby, the job would simply have to go. I resigned, very sadly, and moved into our new house in September. I was pregnant a month afterwards.

'I was determined that this one would succeed - and it did, I'll never know whether cutting out the stress did it in the end, I've no idea, really. I gave up smoking - I'd been a twenty a day person since my twenties, and have never touched a cigarette since. I cut down alcohol, having one or two glasses a week (I'd drunk much more before). I had a nuchal folds scan at seven weeks, and all was well. Then I had an amniocentesis at fourteen weeks - and it was fine. I felt immensely tired all the time, but I tried to do all the right things about food, diet, exercise. I was quite fit from rushing about in my job, so weight wasn't really a problem. I prepared myself by reading lots of books about pregnancy and babies. I went to an antenatal class through my surgery which was helpful in putting me in touch with local women.

'Ben was born at forty-two weeks. It was all very straightforward, really, a vaginal delivery and I went straight for the drugs when it got too painful, I kept feeling it was going to go wrong at the last moment, but it didn't. I remember Henman was playing the last Wimbledon match (it was 1996) and when the pain got too great I screamed: "Turn the bloody TV off, chaps!" It's quite funny, looking back. Ben got a bit stuck coming out and they used forceps. He was still stuck and I began to think: Oh my God this is a bloody nightmare. The doctors said they'd have to do a Caesarian and I screamed no, I didn't want that, unless it was life or death. They said OK, but I'd have to give one last big push. I thought of a strong rugby player hauling his way along a rugby pitch to make his last big try - and out popped Ben. I'd pushed like mad all right.

'John and I felt blissfully happy. We both wanted Ben and we both felt really over the moon about him. I breastfed for nine months and thought I might go back to work, but I haven't. I've really enjoyed motherhood - more than I can possibly describe. Although my old salary would certainly be useful, we have the house as security and we have been quite sensible about money in the past, so we have pensions and securities. Life is tougher now than it was. We're not good at living frugally, and we'll go out and have a bottle of wine with a meal, but we used to live on two expense accounts. It doesn't really matter, not really, because the quality of life is so much greater.

'Ben is a bright child and I've decided to stay home with him full-time until he goes to school. And even then, I'll only work part-time. There's no shortage of things to do locally, as it's very child-centred here. He's got masses of friends from playgroups and I've worked hard at connecting with his cousins. I think my only real regret is that he won't have a brother or sister. I don't really want him to be an only child, but I think he will be, as I'm now forty-eight. The age limit on IVF locally is forty-six and we haven't really looked into it, I suppose, because of all the miscarriages I had. We have considered adoption, but the age limits are against me, too. We're not sure if Ben would thank us for it later because at present we can give him lots of attention as he's only one. It wouldn't be the same if there were two, especially if we adopted an older child who had problems or difficulties. I wouldn't go down the surrogacy road, either, to have another child. I'm not that desperate. So I think it's probably going to be just the one.'

'Ironically, having Ben has made me feel ten years younger, although I'm conscious that I'm older than most of the women I meet at playgroups. I think post-menopause, when I'm at the secondary school gate with grey hair, it might be a bit of a problem. I'd hate to be thought of as a granny at the school gate (although I can always dye the hair): it could be hard on Ben, if I don't think about how to stay relatively young and active. I do make an extra effort to stay in a heathy state as I want to be around for him as long as I can - this means I watch my drinking, diet and don't smoke. I'm much more aware of what my lifestyle can do to me than I would have been in my twenties or thirties. I admit I do have less energy, and so I have to maximise what I've got in order to keep up. I'm going to retrain once Ben goes to school, as I no longer want to be in PR. I couldn't go back at the same level and, anyway, I feel different about it all now. I've thought about doing a history of art or fine arts degree. That would fit in with motherhood well. My guiding principle in life is to be there for Ben, to be there at the school gate to meet him, and to be there in the holidays to enjoy life with him. It's great being a mum at home and not working and I think he's very secure and happy as a consequence. That's good enough for me - at least for now.'

4

Myth 3: Older Bodies Can't Take the Strain

REALITY TODAY: WOMEN HAVE NEVER BEEN FITTER

We're all getting older, it's a fact. From the minute we are born, every minute of every day, in every way, the ageing process is taking its toll. That's part of being human, after all. The desire for immortality and the urge to hold back the natural tide of the ageing process has been a human quest since time began. According to Steven Austad, Associate Professor of Zoology at the University of Idaho, the human race may be able to live well beyond its current lifespan of 120-odd years. He believes the secret to longevity is for women to have children as late in life as possible. Professor Austad specialises in the study of ageing - Gerontology - and he believes that humans could well live to 150, even 200.

It's all down to engineering the right genes. 'Our bodies, or more precisely our genes, have been selected to help us survive long enough to have children and bring them up so that they can do the same,' reports journalist Charles Arthur in the *Independent* in an article entitled, 'Older Mums Do Their Bit for the Human Race', 13 July 1997. 'If people delayed having children until later in life, fewer life-shortening genes (such as the gene that passes on muscular dystrophy, which causes muscle wasting in childhood) would be passed on - because the individual carrying them would die before they could transmit them. Octogenarian parents must have the healthiest set of genes imaginable. Their contribution would mean that humans could live longer and longer.' More research is underway through the Human Genome Project to 'map' virtually every gene in the body so scientists can isolate what really will make us live longer and healthier lives.

Physical effects of late motherhood

When it comes to having a baby over forty, there's no doubt that being older takes its toll on the body. Indeed, Julia Berryman's research at the University of Leicester found that, understandably, 'Older mothers are extremely tired when they have a baby and low energy levels are definitely an issue to be faced.' However, her research also found that 'a lot of younger women also talk about extreme tiredness as well, so low energy does not only afflict older mothers.' Berryman's research found that the younger women are, the more able they are to manage longer hours overall. The younger mothers were more likely to want to sustain a late night lifestyle as well as motherhood, whereas the older mothers were willing to acknowledge their limits and cut back on the social whirl. 'After all, they don't see it as a sacrifice to not go clubbing or drinking, whereas a younger woman may well feel deeply frustrated or ostracised if she doesn't go out on the town,' explains Berryman.

We tend to forget that in the past (until the Pill arrived), women were pregnant for most of their adult lives and well into their forties, when they would have completed their large families. The main difference is that many women will have died not only during childbirth, but from post-partum complications; they also expired simply from being completely worn out by forty or fifty. During the nineteenth century, middle-class women hired nannies and 'wet nurses' to do their childcare (and preserve their own health), while working women kept themselves going on gin, beer and opium-laced medicines which were drunk like water (they also drugged their babies with laudanum and opium to keep them quiet). My own grandmother had my father at forty-seven. He was the youngest of eight children, but it was always rumoured there had been many more (probably eleven) unwanted pregnancies which had been aborted illegally through practical necessity. Women's lives were extremely hard and we easily forget how tough it was to live without contraception, time- and labour-saving household devices and free health care. Today, we live relatively luxurious, affluent, and healthy lives, which is one of the reasons forty is the new thirty for today's woman in mid-life. Fifty can also be the new forty, as Lynne Bezant's story illustrates.

Lynne Bezant: IVF twins at fifty-six

Lynne Bezant became the first woman in Britain to have twins at fifty-six. She and her husband Derek already had three grown-up children. It was reported in the *Mirror* (22 January 2001) that the couple read about other women having babies in their forties and fifties and so they decided to pursue it for themselves. Lynne had suffered two miscarriages previously, plus stillborn twins twenty years ago. Both she and her husband say they never got over their losses. 'When the children left home,' they told *Mirror* reporter Lorraine Fisher, 'we were lonely and longing for more family life. We thought about fostering. But you grow to love the children, then they are taken away from you. That stopped us doing it. Once we'd reached our late forties we realised this was something we were wanting all the time.' They paid to go to the then only clinic in Britain, the London Gynaecological

Clinic, which implants women with donor eggs up until the cut-off age of fifty-five.

Although the Bezants went to the clinic to be assessed when Lynne was fifty-one, they had to wait three years for a donor (not uncommon for women awaiting egg donation). However, the issue of Lynne's fitness was paramount. She had already gone through the menopause and her husband had had a vasectomy by the time she sought out IVF treatment. They discovered his sperm could still be 'recovered' by special means, so they could use his sperm with a donor egg. 'We considered the pros and cons before we did anything about it,' she told the *Mirror,* 'but we're both fit, our families have all lived to a reasonable age, and financially we're relatively stable. I felt that if I could cope with a class of twenty-eight children [she's a teacher], I could cope with youngsters of my own.' Lynne finally found an egg donor a week before she was fifty-six. The eggs were implanted and she became pregnant. She had the babies in June 2001. The media concern about her physical fitness was defended by Professor Ian Craft, who is the head of the clinic where she had the IVF treatment in Harley Street. He was quoted in the *Mirror* (23 January 2001) concerning her physical ability to have twins at fifty-six: 'She is fit, healthy, doesn't smoke or drink and takes plenty of exercise. The medical risks to the babies are relatively small because she has the eggs of a young woman.' Significantly, Professor Craft went on to say, 'I don't understand the fascination people have with age. Lynne will make a far better mother than some women who conceive under the age of eighteen. At the end of the day what does a child need? Loving parents is the answer, and there can be no doubt that this couple deserve these babies and love them.' It is a sign of the times that women are pushing back the boundaries daily to have children later in life - both as the technology improves and their own fitness increases.

Oldest Women to Give Birth

- Oldest woman in Britain to give birth: Elizabeth Adeney (66), 2009 – had a son after IVF, went abroad for treatment (not available in the UK over to women over 50).

- Oldest woman in Britain to have twins: Janet Bosher (58) 2002 – used donated sperm and embryos.

- Oldest mothers in the world: Daljinder Kaur (72) India, 2017 – had her first child after IVF; Maria del Carmen Bousada de Lara (67) Spain, 2006 – gave birth to twin boys after IVF.

Celebrity icons

Of course, we've all got used to images of pampered and rich celebrities in magazines such as *Hello!* and *OK,* where they appear to have pinged back into shape almost the minute the baby is born. Madonna, who had her second child, Rocco, at forty-two, was reported to be back sweating away on her exercise bike only hours after the life-threatening birth. Jane Seymour, who added twins to her family of three at forty-six, looked stick thin and glamorous days, almost, after the birth. These celebrity images can be very damaging to 'ordinary' women's self-esteem and confidence, because there is almost a moral implication that we are 'less than' because we have retained a bit of flab post-baby. We have to remember that these women's fortunes are built on their looks and thus it is essential for them to be glammed up ten seconds after giving birth.

In fact, Kate Winslet, famous for both *Titanic* and for being anti-dieting, blew the gaffe on Hollywood pressure to be perfect by saying she had to lose the weight she put on since having her first baby because: 'I need to work and I won't work again if I don't lose weight.' Any lesser mortal being flanked by personal assistants, personal fitness trainers, a bevy of flunkies, unlimited childcare, and access to the best food, medical care, swimming pools and health farms that money can buy, would probably look pretty fit after having a baby at over forty, too.

Pressure to be Perfect

They both had babies just eight weeks ago, but looking at their svelte, toned figures you'd never guess. Catherine Zeta Jones drew admiring stares when she returned to her home town of Swansea last week, showing off the curves that made her famous in tight, black trousers and a clingy top. And at the LA premiere of her boyfriend Guy Ritchie's film, Snatch, Madonna felt so confident about flaunting her regained figure that she wore a jewelled belt and figure hugging trousers.

From 'How do Celeb Mums Get Flat Tums Just Weeks After Giving Birth?',

Now magazine, October 2000

To some extent celebrity images are iconic in that they push back the boundaries and public perceptions of what a forty-plus woman can be like post-baby, but they are also unreal for most women. We should not beat ourselves up because that kind of bodily perfection is unattainable without a great deal of time, cash, effort and support. Most forty-plus mothers have to make do with a quick weekly swim or a brisk walk to the post office. Those with childcare support, close family or an understanding partner, may well make it to the gym once a week - if they can afford it and can fit it into a busy schedule. It's essential to keep an eye on reality when these celebrity images flood the media because they can be damaging to women's self-esteem if we use them to deride ourselves for being older. The most use they can be is as a role model of what is possible and a spur to getting fit again - over time, in your own way and within your own limited resources.

Body-image mania

In the twenty-first century having a perfect body has almost become a religion. Anorexia, bulimia and other eating disorders have almost reached epidemic proportions and women have never been so obsessed with how they look. We are in the throes of a body-image mania at present, where 'self' is measured by its physical packaging. For any woman, at any age, having a baby is a major challenge. Not least, because your body balloons and it is very easy to pile on the pounds. For younger women this can seem utterly daunting. Most, but not all, are used to being svelte, stylish, able to drop a few pounds whenever they need to, so gaining weight as a baby grows can feel very threatening. As the body's metabolism begins to slow with ageing, it gets harder to shift extra weight. Women in their thirties will find it harder to shift baby fat than their twenty-year old counterparts. It's just a fact of life. Women in their forties will find it very hard to shift baby fat because they may also be dealing with the onset of middle-age spread induced by hormonal changes in the run up to, and during, the menopause.

An important antidote to fearing an increase in body size is developing a more relaxed and self-accepting attitude, which, hopefully, maturity can bring. Julia Berryman's research found that older mothers 'were quite comfortable about their size', even if that size was larger than it had been earlier in life. 'Of course, older mothers took longer to get back in shape than younger, first-time mothers, but the weight-gain difference between 35-plus mothers and 40-plus mothers was minimal. The older mothers had very positive attitudes about their bodies and there was no reason overall why their bodies should not cope extremely well.'

Jo's story: comparing pregnancies in her twenties and forties

Jo does voluntary work for the National Childbirth Trust (NCT) and her story highlights the differences a woman in her twenties might feel about her body, to one in her forties. Jo has been married for twenty-seven years to the same man and lives in Berkshire. Her daughter Elizabeth was sixteen when her mother got pregnant for the second time, completely unexpectedly.

'I was forty-four when I got pregnant again. I had come off the Pill at forty, following my doctor's advice, and I wasn't using any contraception, again on his advice (he denied this later). He was saying at the time that women over a certain age should not be on mini-pills and that pregnancy wasn't really a risk as the menopause was probably coming soon. How wrong he was. We used the 'rhythm method' [having sex on "safe" days when the woman is not ovulating], probably like Cherie and Tony Blair did, and weren't planning a second child at all. I was growing older and getting pregnant wasn't on my mind - until it happened. Then it was a real shock, I can tell you. I thought, "Oh my goodness, I can't be", but I sort of knew straight away that I was. I'm quite tuned in to my body. I missed a period and I was quite sure I was pregnant.

'We didn't tell anybody at first —at least, not outside the family. Elizabeth had got used to being an only child, so it was a real shock to her. I waited until her summer holidays to tell her because I didn't want to disrupt her school exams. I told her quietly and spent time answering her questions. She cried a bit and said, "But Mummy, I like it being just the three of us." When she was younger she'd craved a younger brother or sister, but she'd just got used to things being the way they were. It just didn't occur to her that her elderly parents could have another child (I'm sure she was shocked at the thought that we actually had sex - "Yuk, Mum, how could you?" sort of thing). Anyway, I told her it was OK to feel funny about it and that it was fine to be upset. She did get interested in the pregnancy as things progressed, but she did have a hard time because the dynamics in our family had changed. I also think it was her age and the pressure of her GCSEs.

'I didn't want people to make a fuss because I was older, although they inevitably did. I didn't go anywhere near a midwife until I was five months pregnant, because I didn't want any pressures of any kind. My husband and I discussed the Down's syndrome issue early on and decided just to go with whatever happened. We are Christians and we couldn't have contemplated an abortion from our religious viewpoint. Miscarriage never occurred to me, either. The pregnancy was absolutely fine and the midwife was very understanding about us not wanting tests, even scans. I also told her I could date the baby and she didn't need to do that with a scan. I knew exactly when the baby was conceived. I think she was a bit taken aback, but she noted down my due date. I actually had the baby the day after the due date. I knew a lot about childbirth and my own body, so I felt confident that I was right - something that comes with age and experience, I think.

'I have to say, that although I was older, the second birth was a far better experience. During Elizabeth's birth back in 1979 when I was twenty-eight (which people thought was old for a first baby then), I had been in labour fifteen hours and I had gas and air for the pain. I was exhausted and they gave me pethidine, which I didn't want. After the injection I was unable to push: it made me feel utterly sick and it was a total mistake. I told them, but they wouldn't really listen. The stitches I had after a very bloody forceps delivery were extremely painful and I thought I was going to die! It was really awful. It took me a long time to get over it both physically and emotionally. So with Caitlin I felt I knew a lot more about it all.

'Things are much better now as birth is more woman-centred, even in ordinary hospitals. I knew I had the right to say "no" this time to drugs and to say "I want this" or "I don't want that", without being labelled unreasonable. And

I have to say the delivery was a really positive experience this time. We planned a home delivery - the doctor thought I was mad - but the midwives were confident, and also competent, in doing home deliveries and I planned it all with them. However, I had the same problem as with Elizabeth in that I couldn't push the baby out. I'm only 4' 11", so I guess I'm not strong enough. When we got to the third stage of labour the paramedic flying squad were sent in and I was whisked off to hospital. I didn't argue about it by that stage.

'However, I told them I'd like a ventouse [suction on the baby's head to pull it out] and the registrar said OK, they'd try it. She kept asking me about everything, and explained she would try to do it without cutting me. Then she said "I'm really sorry, but I need to cut you - is that all right?" I told her yes, and to do what she needed to do. I felt I was treated on a very different level and that everything was done in a more consultative way than before. I also used the pain relief I wanted, so I had a TENS machine [electrodes are placed on the skin to control contraction pain by pulsing electrical charges] instead of an epidural or major drugs. I felt I was in control and that I was consulted, and I think the registrar flinched even more than I did when she cut my perineum. She injected me with a local anaesthetic as she did it and kept asking, "Am I hurting you?" and "Is this all right?" She was really very good. It was a far superior experience to Elizabeth's birth and I could really see how the health service had changed its attitudes and practice over twenty years.' Afterwards, I breastfed Caitlin for two years, which was what I wanted. With Elizabeth, I'd been told to do ten minutes each side, which wasn't satisfactory either to her or to me, and indeed, I'd given up at ten months.

'The funniest thing was other people's reactions - which was largely one of shock. People didn't notice I was having a baby, perhaps because people think forty-five-year-old women are a bit plumper anyway. Or maybe they just don't look for it, I don't know. I hid it quite well I think, although the baby felt quite heavy to me. However, even though the birth was much more positive, I did find my body took a longer time to recover. It was a much harder job second time around, because this time, before I was pregnant I was fairly desk-bound, working at computers and doing paperwork. I wasn't as fit as I was during my first pregnancy, when I used to cycle everywhere. I think it took me over two years to shed the weight I gained and I'm not sure my stomach muscles will ever recover- they're pretty shot. However, when Caitlin started at playgroup I decided I had to get fitter as I didn't want to be a blobby, out-of-condition mummy. I started cycling again and going to an aerobics class. I also walked everywhere and left the car at home. I have got arthritis in my hands and that has been a problem. I hadn't been used to holding a baby for a long time and my muscles hurt a lot, but they got better as she got bigger.

'I feel I'm a much better mother to Caitlin (who's now six, I'm fifty-one) than I was to Elizabeth, who is now twenty-two and at university; I'm more child-centred than I was back then, more patient, more laid back and my values have mellowed. I used to shout a lot more than I do now. I think my relationship is closer to Caitlin than it was to Elizabeth, but since she's come along, my husband has got closer to our older daughter. I never wanted to leave Caitlin while I went to work (like I did Elizabeth) and I've spent more time with her just because I want to. Vince earns a good salary in computing so I haven't needed to go out and earn. As a consequence, Caitlin's a real mummy's girl, although Elizabeth now adores her. It's changed her whole view of life and she says she can't wait to have kids of her own. I think I used to be more tired in the early days of Caitlin's life than I am now. The most tiring time was between the years of her being two and three. She was an unexpected blessing - I never expected to have a child in my forties at all - but I have been delighted to find out that I can cope with a young child at my age. I feel fitter than ever and have lots of energy - I think she actually keeps me young.'

Know your body type

Like Jo above, most mothers interviewed for this book admitted to putting on weight and finding that weight harder to shift after forty. However, there were women whose weight dropped fairly quickly, not only through intensive breastfeeding, but because of their natural body type. Women roughly divide into three types: endomorphs, mesomorphs and ectomorphs. Both endomorphs and mesomorphs can find it hard to shift fat, and endomorphs in particular may find weight settling around the hips, bottom, thighs, stomach in the good old British pear-shape and spare-tyre style. However, ectomorphs - the more wiry of the body types - may well find weight returning to normal very quickly (they may even lose weight) after birth, regardless of age.

The women interviewed for this book varied greatly: some put on three stone, while others put on only half a stone; some remained fit and active during pregnancy, while others took to their beds for enforced rest. As with most things, weight gain and fat retention is an entirely individual thing, and thus, although forty-plus women may well have slower metabolisms, it does not necessarily mean that all mothers over forty are going to be Mrs Blobby. What's important to note here - which Julia Berryman's research supports - is that these women may have an easier time psychologically accepting any weight gain, because the child is really wanted and not resented. Also, they have more life experience, self-knowledge and understanding of how their bodies work. Plus, they can also do something about improving their fitness levels after having a baby as they may have more cash and time than their younger counterparts, at least in the long term.

Energy levels

The common myth that 'older bodies can't take the strain' clearly has some credence. Nobody can deny that ageing brings about a loss of energy, elasticity and verve. It would be ridiculous to pretend otherwise. However, there are several factors that should be acknowledged here:

- Energy levels are also a purely individual and subjective thing. Apart from the natural ageing process, there are some women who are simply full of drive, enthusiasm and physical energy because of their genetic make-up, personality and body type. Some women are simply 'on the go' all the time and like to be busy, busy, busy. These women may be the very ones who can contemplate having a baby forty plus because they have spent their lives rushing about.

- Energy levels are very much affected by diet and there has never before been so much information about what makes our bodies tick - and tick well. Magazines like *Top Sante, Health & Beauty* are packed with useful information and advice about eating healthily. Most newspapers now have a weekly health section aimed at women, advocating a low-fat, high-fibre diet, packed with fresh fruit and vegetables (preferably organic). It's hard to ignore the fact that five portions of fruit and veg a day, plus lean chicken, fish, or pulses, and complex carbohydrates, such as potatoes, brown rice, wholewheat pasta and bread, will boost our energy. It's also important to drink at least eight glasses of water a day to flush out damaging toxins.

- Energy levels are affected by everyday addictions and often women find themselves giving up smoking, cutting down on drinking alcohol, watching their diets by forty because their bodies can't take the abuse that they might have been able to endure in their twenties. Women often wryly comment about this, but the desire to stay young and fit can translate itself into good health practice for forty-plus mothers. My book *Overcoming Addiction: Positive Steps to Break Free from Addiction and Build Self-Esteem* may be of help in this area.

- Energy levels are boosted by good, old-fashioned sleep. Although we need less sleep as we get older, there is nothing like a restorative night's sleep to help older mothers recover from the rigours of the day. It's also advisable not to drink alcohol before bedtime as it actually disturbs sleep patterns, but to have a warm (low-fat) milky drink, a soporific herbal remedy or to burn lavender oil in the bedroom, to relax. Getting enough sleep will definitely help an older mother cope better with the stresses of looking after a young child, particularly as they usually tend to come bouncing into the parental bedroom in the early hours.

- Energy levels are also boosted by regular, gentle exercise, such as yoga, swimming, walking, or more strenuous and aerobic exercise, such as fitness classes (like step aerobics), a workout at the gym, using weights, dancing, cycling, or ancient disciplines, such as T'ai Chi. Even ordinary daily chores, like housework, shopping and gardening, can keep women fit. Older women are encouraged to keep fit these days as a way of coping well with the menopause and of increasing bone density, in order to combat conditions such as osteoporosis (thinning bones). Older mothers who keep fit will also be doing themselves a favour as they move into their fifties and beyond.

- Energy levels can be increased by the use of alternative remedies and treatments. Acupuncture, acupressure, homoeopathy, Shiatsu, reiki, aromatherapy massage are easily available and affordable today. A wide range of dietary supplements such as co-enzyme Q10, ginseng, kelp, multivitamins - Esther-C, for instance - can increase health and welfare. You should always consult a GP or pharmacist when taking any preparation - especially if you are going to try to get pregnant, are pregnant or are breastfeeding (there are certain vitamins, like vitamin A, which can actually damage a foetus, so it's important to check first).

There are plenty of women's health magazines available apart from *Top Sante Health & Beauty,* such as *Women's Health, Fitness, Pregnancy Magazine,* and *Mother and Baby,* which give detailed and up-to-date information about health, exercise and diet. A good book to dip into is *Women's Bodies, Women's Wisdom: The Complete Guide to Women's*

Health and Wellbeing by Dr Christiane Northrup (Piatkus). Most newspapers also carry special health columns aimed at women, such as Femail in *the Daily Mail,* and the Women's page in the *Guardian.* There are also lots of online resources; just make sure they are genuine. Women's health has never been so well researched and reported on and any woman who wants to improve her health forty plus has plenty of information available to her today. This applies to women across class and circumstance, as it is perfectly possible to boost energy and health even within a tight budget and time schedule. It just takes some planning and determination (and a fair smidgeon of luck).

Iman's Tips on Getting Your Body Back

Model Iman, then forty-five, had baby Zahra with the late pop icon David Bowie, then fifty-three, in August 2000. Voted one of the most beautiful women in the world, Iman was asked by Hello! magazine about her fitness post birth: 'I think I'm going to have to wait a while before I get back into the exercise regime I usually do. It's a strenuous workout and I need to wait another six weeks or so, and then just do gentle stuff which will gradually increase to a hard daily workout. I'm quite insufferable about fitness, I suppose: I find my weight is coming down slowly and fairly naturally. Though I can't wait to get back into the gym. The one thing you learn as you get older is that the body will do what the body wants. All you can do is try to guide it a little.'

Hello! magazine, September 2000

Zoe's story: optimising her health to have a baby at forty-four

Zoe, a photographic stylist, is now fifty and has been married to Tim, a photographer, for twenty-five years. They had a daughter, Sophie, when she was thirty-six.

'We had spent years struggling in the photography trade and we didn't have much money, so we waited a long time to try for our first baby. Although the pregnancy was fine, the birth was absolutely terrible. I had no pain relief for sixteen hours - the entire duration of my labour. It was thoroughly unpleasant, although totally wonderful to have Sophie in my arms afterwards. Despite the birth, I knew I wanted another child and being in my late thirties by then, I knew I'd have to get on with it.

'However, I found it much harder trying to get pregnant the second time around. My fertility had dropped and from thirty-nine to forty-three I ended up paying for fertility treatment. It was a terrible time and put my relationship under a lot of pressure. Each month I would have hormone injections, which were very painful and unpleasant, and then I'd get my hopes up, only to have them dashed. It was also very expensive as IVF and IUF (In Utero Fertilisation) cost about £2000 per monthly treatment back then. I desperately wanted another child and I got more desperate as I went on. I'm one of five children, and my mother was one of sixteen (I've got fifty-one cousins), so I was convinced I'd be able to conceive again. But I was aware of my age, and felt forty-four would be far too old to be a new mum. I felt very upset not to have another child, but gradually resigned myself to the fact. Anyway, life was good, work was coming in faster and Sophie, Tim and I were very happy. Finally, I decided to give away all the baby clothes. I cried a great deal, but felt it was all over. I was forty-three.

'Then, to my utter amazement, I became pregnant. I couldn't believe it. It's true what they say about taking your eye off the ball. Ironically, I now had a lot of mixed feelings about it. A lot of fear, for one, because I knew that I would find it physically difficult and I was worried about being forty-four when the baby was born. However, I have to say that the second pregnancy and birth were an absolutely wonderful experience. I'd been so put off hospitals by

Sophie's birth that I decided to do things differently this time and take charge of both my health and the birth. I never worried about Down's syndrome or miscarriage, so I simply focused on positive things, like using herbal remedies and yoga to boost my health. I did have some water retention towards the end of the pregnancy, but I hired an independent midwife (the best money I've ever spent, about £1300 back then) and a birthing pool. I resisted all tests and didn't have scans, but I took extremely good care of myself. I watched what I ate, didn't drink or smoke (I don't smoke anyway), and my weight gain was minimal.

'Toby was finally born at forty-two weeks at home. It was the most wonderful, positive experience to float in warm water and marvellous to give birth lying on my side. My husband and mother were there and we all held Toby minutes after he was born. Even though I had a little perineal tear, it healed beautifully with the help of herbal baths.

'Toby is now six and the age gap between Toby and Sophie (she's now fourteen) hasn't been a problem, although she was naturally a little resentful at first. Of course, the juggling act of being a mother and professional is hard to balance and I do feel tired and go to bed early a lot. But most mothers find it hard to get the balancing act right, whatever their age. I went back to work part-time at about three months after Toby, but working from home part-time is a real boon. I do feel older mothers have wisdom on their side and we're not so stressed out under crisis, or as competitive or pushy as younger mothers. I suppose the main downside is not having the stamina. I can't play football with Toby and can't run (I have wonky knees), but I don't really come up against ageism because there are a lot of older mothers in my part of North London. I still take care to keep myself healthy, still do yoga and watch my diet. It's important for me to optimise my health not only for my children, but for myself. My children are my number one priority and even though I work, I love having time to talk to my children as we walk to school. We have a really good relationship which I put down, to a great extent, to my age. Older is definitely better.'

Iman's Tips for Older Mothers

'Make sure your decision to have a child is based on the need to share your life completely with another little human being and not because of some personal need for validation as a woman. The child must come first above all else. And pace yourself every day. There is quite a lot you will have to give up. You won't be popping out to the corner cafe for a nice romantic dinner as often as you used to, and the cinema or the theatre will start to be a nice memory, at least for the first couple of years. In short, you'll never have seen so much of the inside of your home as you now will. But the up side ... oh, I can't begin to tell you!'

Hello! magazine, September 2000

5

Myth 4: Disabled Women Over Forty Can't Have Children

REALITY TODAY: DISABLED MOTHERS OVER FORTY ARE PERFECTLY ABLE

'I was visiting hospital having varicose veins treated when, during the examination, I mentioned my periods were irregular. I was also putting on weight, which I could not shed. When he examined me, the doctor mentioned I might have a cancerous growth and I was very worried. They did a urine sample and then did another examination and I was told I was twenty-three weeks pregnant! I was forty-three years old and had three sons, the youngest being 17 at the time. I went home and told my husband, who was delighted, and we opened a bottle of champagne. The next day we went back to hospital and saw the heartbeat and everything was fine from then on, including a normal birth. That was twenty years ago - and we have a beautiful daughter who is a complete joy to us. We adore her and she is a lovely person. Having a baby at forty-three was the most wonderful thing in my life - cancer would certainly not have been.'

Letter to me at *Home & Life* magazine, September 2000

There are, of course, many women like myself, who are not only over forty, but who are disabled in some way as well. Few of us reach our forties without having some kind of mild disability, such as a bad back or failing eyesight.

However, a woman who is already living with disabilities of some kind (i.e. chronic illness) or who is registered disabled, will have to handle the double whammy of being older and physically disadvantaged. It obviously depends on the type and level of disability how much this may impair a woman's ability to conceive. There are many women who experience gynaecological disabilities, such as endometriosis or fibroids, and who have no idea how much their condition is affecting their lives until they try to conceive (see the chapters on Myth 1 and Myth 3). One woman in her forties I spoke to - who has remained childless after years of trying for a child - has suffered severe endometriosis to the point that it has really limited her life. She has had to work part-time, rest each month before, during and after her period because she experiences great pain, take care over her diet, not drink alcohol, and, in the end, has had to accept that she probably won't be able to have children. Her case is very sad and probably not uncommon. However, it is inspiring to acknowledge that some fortunate women, such as Rebecca (see below), have been able to have babies in their forties despite years of serious gynaecological problems.

Rebecca's story: overcoming disabling gynaecological problems to have a baby at forty

Rebecca, now forty-five, runs her own PR business from home. She is married to Trevor, forty-six, and they have a gorgeous son, James, who is four. James is a 'miracle' baby to them both.

'I'd been written off by one set of doctors as someone who would never be able to conceive,' Rebecca explains candidly, 'because my womb had been virtually ripped to pieces by having a copper 7 coil inserted during my twenties. I had had a pregnancy at twenty-three when I was at university. It was the wrong time of my life, with the wrong partner, and I had a termination. It was a difficult decision, but I knew it would have been disastrous to go ahead. Afterwards, I had a coil fitted as I didn't want to be on the Pill, for health reasons. However, the coil completely screwed up my insides. It was horrendous. I got married soon after this to a man who turned out to be manic-depressive. I assumed we would have children - we both said we wanted them - but I had all these physical problems from the coil. I spent about four months of the first year of our marriage being in and out of hospital, having my fallopian tubes blown through with blue dye, taking piles of antibiotics. I was told I probably would never be able to conceive again, which was very tough.

'Nonetheless, though perhaps naively, I assumed my first husband and I would try for children, despite the obvious difficulties. We went on holiday to Kenya and suddenly he declared he didn't want any. He said he'd changed his mind largely because he saw himself being displaced by a child in my affections. He was terribly frightened he wouldn't be the centre of my attention any more. From then on the relationship went downhill. We hardly ever slept together (I would use a diaphragm if we did) and in the end we split up. By then he was doing large quantities of cocaine and booze, and only seemed to drag me down psychologically. I lost a lot of confidence and it took about three years for me to regain enough self-esteem to feel I was worthy of having another relationship.

'By then my career had really begun to take off. I had decided on advertising and I worked for a top agency gaining fabulous business experience. I worked hard and got promoted. I had to pay for the mortgage on our house on my own (my husband had moved out by then), and my husband demanded quite a lot of money as part of the divorce settlement. However, I bought him out for peace of mind.

'I still wanted children as I entered my thirties, but it looked further away than ever, especially with my continuing physical problems and a failed marriage behind me. Therefore I threw everything into my career. I went into therapy and soon realised I had been going for relationships which were dead end and doomed to failure. And then I met

Trevor. It was a Saturday and I was going shopping. I didn't want to go to a lunch party I'd been invited to, but thought I should pop in. (Trevor was in the same frame of mind.) I was not dressed properly or made up. But we met (the lunch was at a mutual friend's) and we talked and talked all afternoon. I knew he was special and asked my friend to make sure he got my number. I was thirty-seven, but I was very wary of getting involved at that time. However, a week later, we ended up having an intense weekend together.

'Everything was accelerated by the fact that my father died suddenly soon afterwards. I was in total shock and Trevor was a wonderful support. His were the arms I fell into, both literally and metaphorically, after my dad died. I suddenly realised how much I loved him - a moment of pure realisation - and that I wanted his child. However, I had also been offered a top job in Eastern Europe and I had taken it, without telling Trevor. It was only a month after my father died when Trevor asked me to marry him. We were walking along a pavement in Cornwall when he said, "Are you going to marry me, then?" And I said, "Pardon, where's the grazed knee and the rose between your teeth?" He said, "Listen, you don't know how hard it is to ask you." I apologised and thought about it afterwards and I gave him my answer - yes - in a Christmas card. Two weeks later I left the country for the Eastern Europe office and Trevor came with me to settle me in.

'We spent a year having a commuting relationship between our countries. I was earning shedloads of money, so I could pay for a lot of travel. We saw each other every two weeks and really learned to trust each other. It was a wonderful time, we had a great laugh and lots of fantastic experiences. We eventually got married at the end of 1994. I was thirty-nine. As I was earning obscene amounts of money we decided Trevor should stop working and come and join me. We had used contraception up until this point as, oddly, even though I thought babies were an impossibility, I nonetheless didn't want to take a chance with my career. By now, though, I did want a baby - absolutely.

'Because I had been told I couldn't have one, it just seemed there was no harm in trying. I didn't think it would happen because I still had so many gynaecological problems. I had two laparoscopics to check me out and discovered I had nine fibroids, one of which was the size of a tangerine. I had a myomectomy, which removed them. I also had endometriosis and adenomyosis, which meant my womb had a strange, dripping lining which stopped eggs adhering. I thought I would never, ever get pregnant with all this to deal with. However, the day we got married, I stopped using contraception, and within five months, I was pregnant. I had actually done my research and had booked an appointment with Lord Winston, the great fertility expert. So when we walked into his London office, I was already pregnant and he brusquely told us not to bother him as we'd done it all on our own. He referred us to "one of his men", Philip Bennet, who was absolutely wonderful. He's the funniest guy I've ever met in the medical profession - whizzing to work on his girlfriend's Harley Davidson.

'I really couldn't believe I had got pregnant. It was an utter and complete surprise - and a miracle. I did the pregnancy test again because I just couldn't take it in. From the first day, I was also convinced I was going to lose the baby. I really didn't think I deserved to get that lucky after all I had been through. I remember at seven weeks I had one rush to the toilet when I thought I might lose the baby, but it was fine. I felt very exhausted all the time.

'We still lived abroad and luckily the doctor was not at all worried about my age. She knew all about my history, but she adopted a totally positive attitude about it all, which was very reassuring.' She said my womb was very scarred - from the copper 7 and my fibroids, and I had an anterior (low lying) placenta, which could be a problem during birth. But she made sure I had excellent treatment. However, I was told that if I went into natural labour there was a 100 per cent chance the baby would die, and a 70 per cent chance I would die. That scared both Trevor and me, I can tell you. So I knew I would have to have an elective Caesarian. That was OK.

'The other problem I experienced throughout my pregnancy, was the excruciating pain I had. The adhesions in my womb felt like someone was twisting and turning a knife whenever the baby moved. I would double up in pain and nearly faint. Sometimes I didn't think I could endure the pain, but I did. Meanwhile, we were packing up our home and my office in Eastern Europe and returning to England. At thirty-seven and a half weeks, I stopped work and we both spent time pottering around my old house (which I'd rented out while abroad), painting the nursery together.

'I still didn't really believe it would be all right in the end. I couldn't let myself. However, the Caesarian was absolutely wonderful. I'd been in agony six or seven times a day, so it was a great relief to get the baby out. James was born to the sound of Mozart's flute and harp concerto. It was a lovely, positive experience and Trevor was there throughout. We took the baby home after a few days in hospital and he slept straight through the night immediately. Breastfeeding was easy - and I did it for nine months. I managed to go for a two mile walk only nine days after coming out of hospital. We were so happy that James was fine, that I was still alive, and that we'd got there in the end. I recovered fairly well and we even went round the world when James was two - to Australia, New Zealand, Fiji, Hawaii. I love deep-sea diving and James was pulled along in his buggy by a rope on the jetty at four months, while I dived in Scapa Flow between breastfeeds.

'I believe that the wealth of experience that you gain as a grown-up before you have a child can be refocused towards your child, for his benefit as well. Instead of displacing yourself for a number of years while he's young - and not being able to be you - I think it's crucial to carry on being yourself. Otherwise, you can use your child as an excuse not to get on with things - it's a very convenient excuse, of course. It depends on how focused you want to be. Anyway, James is used to travelling and he sees me as being very active - even though I'm now forty-five. I am currently trying for another baby, although I'm not sure if it will happen. We both want another, but are aware it's a real outside chance. I do regret I didn't start on all this earlier, seeing as I actually was able to have a child in the end, but you can't change history, can you? I don't smoke, hardly drink, take my folic acid and cod liver oil against my arthritic joints and we have sex at the right time of the month and stay with my bottom raised up in the air for an hour or longer to aid conception afterwards (I've even stayed like that all night, believe me). But who knows if it will ever happen again? However, I think we'll have a cut-off point in a year, when I'm forty-six-and-a-half. We may consider adoption, I don't know. But whatever happens, I feel - we both feel - that we're probably the most lucky parents in the whole world.'

Don't give up hope too soon

The myth Rebecca's story clearly challenges here is the notion that if you are forty plus, with disabling gynaecological problems, you should simply give up on the idea of having children. But you just never know how things may turn out - until you try. My own GP told me 'not to bother' when I first went to her at forty saying I wanted to try for a baby. I think she looked at my pile of notes, including the history of asthma and serious RTA (road traffic accident), and felt overwhelmed by the challenge. I changed my doctor, not my desire to have a baby.

Clearly, there are women who have managed to have a baby - as I have - who have faced the most enormous challenges physically, but who, nonetheless, have gone on to be perfectly able mothers, like Rebecca above. This doesn't mean to say they don't have to take extra care with their health or recruit additional support, but it does mean that motherhood can be possible for women who might be written off by health professionals or peers.

Becoming disabled after having a baby at forty plus

Of course, it can all happen the other way round. If women have gynaecological problems, like Rebecca, at least they can prepare themselves both physically and psychologically as they approach late motherhood. However, if disability hits a woman *after* birth, it can be doubly debilitating.

Some women may think they are perfectly healthy when they get pregnant over forty, only to find out otherwise after the birth. Obviously, this can be a real shock, especially as it will probably entail a total life change, not only from having a baby, but also from dealing with a disability. Such women will need extra help and support to cope - physically, financially, practically and emotionally. Disability can occur through all sorts of means - heart attacks or strokes, blindness, car, train or plane crashes, natural or civil disasters, or simply through chronic illnesses, like cancer. Nobody is ever really prepared for becoming disabled, and we tend to take physical ability for granted. We even abuse ourselves regularly with alcohol, cigarettes, drugs and food, without really thinking how it may affect us long term. Should a woman become severely ill or disabled having had a baby, she will not only be unprepared for the shock, but will certainly find the job challenging, as Marion's story illustrates.

Marion's story: becoming disabled over forty after having a baby

Marion, who is now forty-five, hasn't worked since 1992. She gave up work deliberately to increase her chances of getting pregnant. 'I didn't get married until I was thirty-five. I worked as an accountant solidly through my twenties and thirties and only when I was made redundant (the company moved to another city), did I think about having a baby. As I approached forty I felt that if I didn't do it soon, I'd never do it. It didn't really matter until then, I don't think.

'I was actually very close to my own mother - who is German - and who had me when she was forty-five and my father was fifty. I have elder brothers who are twelve and thirteen years older than me, so I suppose it wasn't a strange idea for me to try to get pregnant in my forties; I wasn't really aware of my mother's age when I was a child. Someone did say to me my granny was waiting for me at the school gate one day - and it turned out to be my mother. I simply explained my grandparents were dead (they died during the war) and didn't take it as a slight. I never had grandparents myself and you don't necessarily miss what you haven't had. At least, not unless you have a bad relationship with your parents. But mine was good, at least with my mother (my father was a bit more distant).

'When I married, my husband wanted children, but equally didn't want to push me into it. I think being older means that you appreciate that having a child is going to be a completely life-changing event and I've always been very scathing of people who carry on their lives as if they haven't got a child. When they say "we do whatever we used to do, we go to restaurants" and so on I'm somewhat disapproving. Why have a child if you want life to carry on as it was before? Personally, I was worried about the changes a child would inevitably bring. It's not that we go to nightclubs, pubs and restaurants, it's more about having less time for yourself, and to do what you want. I was aware this would be the case.

'I think reaching forty focuses the mind, because you don't know when the biological clock is going to stop. You really don't know the very hour it will stop, that's the point. I thought it would take years to get pregnant when we stopped using contraception, but it was only six months. Not really a long enough time for me to think about it being a problem. I had a very fatalistic approach at that time. I didn't want to explore IVF or anything, I thought it would either happen or it wouldn't. And it did. Anyway, the pregnancy lasted only twelve weeks and then I miscarried. I remember it was over the Christmas and New Year period, and we were laughing a lot at a Schwarzennegger film called *Kindergarten Cop*, when

I started to bleed. It was a "missed abortion" in that the baby had died probably around six weeks, but hadn't miscarried at the time. I didn't burst into tears, I was quite matter-of-fact. I think I felt quite fatalistic about that as well: it just wasn't meant to be. I was not going to have an amniocentesis, I'd already decided that, so I felt there was probably something seriously wrong with the baby.

'One of my older brothers is slightly mentally handicapped and I have no illusions that some handicapped people are not particularly pleasant. I'm sorry to say so, but I can't stand my brother and he's not a particularly nice person. He's selfish and greedy and not very likeable. I think, consequently, I was deeply frightened of having a disabled child. And probably that's one of the reasons I left it so late. Anyway, we decided to carry on trying and I was pregnant six months later.

'I felt nauseous only for one day, otherwise I was fine. I felt very uncomfortable towards the end of the pregnancy, when there was no room for expansion, which gave me rib pain. I'm only five foot, so it was a bit of a squeeze in there. I was worried about the child, she came ten days early, when I was thirty-eight and a half weeks pregnant, and I was relieved that she was OK. I had a fairly easy birth. My waters broke when I was sitting watching a film. I sat on a piano stool backwards, leaning on the sofa, and couldn't get comfortable. Then I went to bed, but kept jumping out every six or seven minutes with contractions. I hadn't even packed my bag or got a nursery ready. We hadn't bought anything yet, like clothes or nappies. I don't know why, I just never thought it would be real, somehow. Anyway, we phoned the hospital who said get in the bath for a few hours, and I said, "No, I'm coming in." I felt the birth was nearer than that.

'In fact, Elizabeth was born at 6 a.m., only four hours after we got to hospital. I nearly strangled my husband, clinging on to the T-shirt round his neck while I gulped gas and air. I wanted an epidural but the midwife said that it was "too late for all that". The pain was intense at the time, but over relatively quickly. I was just hugely relieved she was out, and I breastfed immediately.

'The first three weeks were the worst as we all adjusted. I was very tired. I did get depressed a bit with lack of sleep, a constantly crying baby, pooey nappies. I didn't know what to do and we weren't really prepared, I suppose, because I hadn't believed it would really happen. A short time afterwards, I began to get tingling up my leg when I walked. It got worse and worse and it would tingle if I moved my head, and I felt weird. I saw a doctor and mentioned it and he sent me for an MRI scan [Magnetic Resonance Imaging is a procedure that is used for obtaining multiple cross-sectional pictures of parts of the body in order to look for abnormalities]. I was told, then and there, that I had MS - multiple sclerosis. I couldn't really take it in. I took my mother-in-law with me on that momentous hospital visit to look after the baby and the neurologist told me the truth; he said he wouldn't have told me if I hadn't had someone to support me that day. I was very upset and frightened; what would happen to me? To the baby? Would I die? They said it was too early to tell any of that.

'I had noticed tingling in my limbs for ages, but had never really paid it proper attention. As far back as eight years ago, I remembered tingling sensations, but they seemed to escalate after the birth. Perhaps because I was tired, I don't know. I've got a very slow type of MS, quite benign, really. Nonetheless, it's hard to live with, knowing it will get worse and worse. I'm finding walking much more difficult now and I'm quite lame.

'Over the last four years things have got progressively worse. When my daughter was a few weeks old, I wanted to go to a big shop which was only twenty minutes away. I took the pushchair. Now I wouldn't even contemplate it. When the MI5 building was blown up in London all the buses were stopped. I didn't realise this, and I set off for school with my daughter. We walked and that was fine, but coming back there were no buses and I spent a long time sitting down on people's front walls and resting. I was in tears and spent the rest of the day in bed, resting. The effort finished me off, totally. I think I do get tired disproportionately - which is coupled with being over forty. My husband takes Elizabeth to the park and he can run around and play with her. I can't get up slopes or move fast, so I can't join in. When she was small, she refused to use reins and another mother had to run after her when she ran off, thinking it was a game. But I'm able to do things with her like drawing, painting, writing and reading. I've hired a cleaner, as house work is far too heavy and anyway, I'd rather spend time with Elizabeth.

'I think I can be a bit short-tempered with her because I'm very tired. I am sad I'm not as physically able as I used to be, too. My husband would have dearly loved a second child, but I don't think I could cope with a small baby making demands. No sleep, or disrupted sleep, would be very difficult for me now. I want to look after my daughter properly and what energy I have I give to her. My daughter doesn't really comment on my illness rather, she says, "Mummy doesn't walk very well." She's very understanding and takes me for who I am. I've put on a lot of weight with MS, which I don't like. But there's not a lot I can do about it. As for my old life - I have no real desire to go back out to work.

'I don't believe in "quality time". I think children may not want "quality time" at 7 p.m. when they're tired. They'd rather have time with you when they need it. I feel I've "been there" and "done that" regarding big corporations and earning good money. I did that for fourteen years. I'm good at saving and I've amassed a fair amount of money, so we are fairly secure. The trick is not to spend it, I've found.

'I think I expect and demand more of my husband now I have MS. I think he gets it in the neck, somewhat. We have a good, sound relationship, however, and he's stuck with me through it. We've been married ten years and I feel Elizabeth has been a good addition to our relationship. Although things are tough, I've always made a big effort to ensure that Elizabeth mixes with other children. My diary is her diary, my friends have come from her friends and we've always got someone coming round to visit. I think my friends are really child-centred people and I've lost touch with the single people or childless people I used to mix with. The best thing about being a mother over forty, regardless of my disability, is that I've got time for my child. I know this time will never be repeated and that she'll be gone in her teens. Or maybe I will be, who knows? Life throws things at you and you have to deal with them. I just relish every minute of the time we spend together now.'

***

Marion's story is clearly a tough one. Not only is she coping with a degenerative disease over forty, but she has a young child to care for. However, she made it clear to me that although she finds life hard, it was far better for her to have Elizabeth than not, because she has a focus for her life and a spur to keep as fit and active as she can be. With a supportive husband, good friends and additional social service and household help, it has been perfectly possible to be an able (if tired) parent. She loves her daughter and has time for her, which counts for a lot.

Wisely, Marion has made provision by setting up trust funds, guardianship agreements, and life insurance, so that should she (or her husband) die early, Elizabeth will be cared for until adulthood. All parents worry about dying early and forty-year-olds are obviously nearer the end of the expected life-span than their twenty-year-old counterparts, but they may actually have the foresight, financial security, knowledge and skill to put money-saving plans into action, in order to protect their young. Younger parents may well leave it until later, because of the need for a good cash flow in the present, but they can still become disabled or die before their time, leaving their children completely unprotected.

Overcoming disability

Some women have to decide whether they will try to have a baby when they are already disabled. Of course, this depends on the level and nature of disability, the type of woman and her life circumstances. It has to be an entirely individual decision, although with certain genetically transmitted disabilities the choice will be a very hard one to make. Disabled women have usually been discounted as mother material, whether it is brittle bones or cystic fibrosis that they have to live with. We have all sorts of prejudices which still play out in society about which disabilities are acceptable and which are not. To some people, the very idea that disabled people will be sexually active at all is anathema, particularly when there is mental impairment involved. However, some disabled women may only be able to have a baby over forty, as in Caroline's inspiring case.

Caroline's story: overcoming disability to have a baby at forty-one

Caroline is now forty-five, living with her partner Ian, fifty-three and their son Robin, a very energetic four-year-old. Caroline's health has never been better. Of course, she's tired, like any other parent, who works part-time, and she has to take extra care to look after herself when she is under stress so that she keeps well. Caroline's amazing story is a testament to the possibility of overcoming chronic, even life-threatening, physical disabilities and being able to have a perfectly happy, healthy child at over forty.

'I spent most of my thirties being weighed down by different health problems,' she explains, 'and I thought I'd never, ever manage to have a child. I first wanted a baby back in my twenties and I actually left a serious love relationship because the guy didn't want to have a child with me. I was working in a women's refuge at the time and ran the crèche. I found I loved the aliveness, the passion and playfulness of children and began to really want to have my own child. I was about twenty-five when I realised I was very lonely and would never feel complete without having a child myself. But my then partner was terrified of children and didn't want kids (he'd had a terrible childhood himself and that had put him right off). He didn't want to face the difficulties.

'Then I was in relationships with women for a while. It was part of working for a women's refuge in a way, because we saw the worst side of men. It was very harrowing working there and I think we sought solace from each other. I'm probably bisexual and have always been attracted to women I feel very close to. But it was also part of the Zeitgeist of the time (it was the 1970s), and I wondered if I'd ever feel that close to men. Women seemed easier, somehow (I still feel this to some extent).

'Anyway, my first serious illness started when I was twenty-nine. After leaving the refuge I got involved with Craig, who was working in Nicaragua as a charity worker and it was an important, new relationship. I visited him in Nicaragua and we knew we'd probably live together, possibly even have children. I was very physically active and involved in campaigning work, until I was struck down by ME (myalgic encephalomyelitis - also known as chronic fatigue syndrome). I got really sick with it for eighteen months. It was a terrible time. I had to be in a darkened room for about twenty-two hours a day. I couldn't stand light so I couldn't watch TV, or read. I couldn't go out. One day I tried to set off for the local shops and I felt I was gradually melting into the pavement. I couldn't put one foot in front of the other and couldn't see how I would possibly get home again. The whole world was swimming about me. The worst aspect was dreadful exhaustion - it was very frightening. I also couldn't sleep properly as day and night sort of rolled into one.

'I had to give up my job which I loved. Then I moved into my brother's house and relied on good friends to support me, although I wasn't very good at taking help because I was a fiercely independent person. My boyfriend returned from Nicaragua to live with me, and I don't think he'd realised how sick I was - I'd hidden it from him to some extent. Our relationship was under strain and he would come home from work and say, "I'm only getting the dregs of you." He also found out that his last girlfriend was pregnant and was going to have the baby. So he had to cope with being a new dad with a woman with whom he'd just finished. I found that hard because I wanted a baby with him - and there he was having one with someone else.

'I tried to get a new job, but couldn't cope with it easily. I retrained in computing, but my memory was poor and I was very debilitated. It felt like I wasn't living in my own mind. Overall, it took me ten years to get over ME, from twenty-nine to thirty-nine. A very long haul. I occasionally get relapses when I am under stress or unhappy, but it is very, very rare these days and I know what to do about it (rest, have acupuncture, eat well, get connected with people who love me, and so on). And in the meantime I got cancer. I think this was linked with ME in some way, as I got lymphomas (cancer of the lymph glands) under my eyelids. I was at the hairdressers when I found them. I was still feeling very tired with the ME symptoms and my eyes were hurting. I pulled back an eyelid, looked in a mirror and saw this thing growing under my eyelid. I'd wondered why one of my eyelids was drooping a bit. In fact, I'd got growths around both eyes. However, the first doctor said I shouldn't make a fuss and it was nothing to worry about. Subsequently, she got the sack (they even wrote to me to tell me).

'My eyes continued to hurt and six months later I was referred to Bart's in London. The consultant was so excited when he saw my eyes he was jumping up and down, calling to people, wanting to take pictures. The first biopsy was negative so I was sent away. The second biopsy was done because the growths kept coming back. I had it done without anaesthetic which was a real mistake. I overheard a conversation between two doctors discussing my lymphomas and freaked out. They never told me directly that I had cancer or explained anything so I was very shocked and upset. However, I then had to have radiotherapy on my eyes which was horrendous. I had to go every day for three weeks. It was frightening because they put lead contact lenses in my eyes, which hurt, then put me in a concrete room and zapped me with radiotherapy. I felt terrible and ill, I hadn't recovered from ME and now I felt sick with radiotherapy. My eyes were like red raw meat. I had to wear diving goggles afterwards and my eyelashes, hair and eyebrows fell out. I'd go into work (I had a new computing job) in diving goggles, with black pen marks all over my face, and had to sit at my computer with people staring at me while I felt sick and exhausted. Craig and I weren't getting on by now and I moved in with a good woman friend. The relationship with Craig ended, although eventually he became a friend.

'The radiotherapy worked and gradually I got better from both illnesses. Part of getting well led me into a sexy affair with Andrew, whom I'd met in computing. It was a light-hearted, fun relationship which was what I needed at the time. It really made me relax about my illnesses. However, the cap I used failed and I got pregnant. Andrew was absolutely horrified, not least because in the very same week another girlfriend announced she was pregnant, too. I wasn't going to see him for dust, obviously.

'I'd bought my own flat after I'd left Craig and I contemplated lone parenthood. I really wanted the baby, but wasn't confident that I could cope alone as I was still recovering from my illnesses. Physical exhaustion and mental confusion still plagued me. I contacted the social services and asked whether they could offer home help support if I went ahead with the pregnancy. They said no. I really did want the child, but I felt very anxious and was having terrible morning sickness. Reluctantly, I decided on a termination. I still mourn that baby - she would have been thirteen by now - and each year I mark the day of her death. Then my beloved granny died and I felt - "how much more can I take?" Andrew disappeared and I was very angry with him at the time. Then he reappeared and we had a sexual relationship of sorts again - and I got pregnant. Again it was a failed cap - I didn't want to use the Pill or the coil because of my health problems. This time he was more supportive of the pregnancy - I was in my mid-thirties by now - but I miscarried at eight weeks. Again it was devastating. I wrote a poem about it:

> A kiss of life
> whispered within me.
> You grew,
> a soft crystal ball of
> delicate tissue.
>
> But now
> rich, thick life blood
> trickles and drips.
> Red tear drops
> tear my dark heart,
> as you die
> inside me.

'I can still cry, thinking about those lines. The relationship was always on and off with Andrew and then he met a woman with teenage children and that was that - he was off.

'I spent time alone after this. I worked hard as a computer expert for a charity and got healthy. I decided I wasn't going to have children, I gave up hope. I was single and I felt I'd never find a man, or the right man. Then I met Ian at a work conference. In fact, I'd met him several years earlier and he'd been interested in me back then, but I'd discounted him as he was married. This time, when we met, I was getting well and it was obvious his marriage was ending. I thought he was a lovely man. I'd been feeling very lonely and single, on the shelf even, and that my emotional life was over. I felt warmed, heartened, touched by how much he loved me and I felt very close to him as our affair blossomed. He wasn't the sort of man I ever would have fancied before, but our relationship grew.

'The baby question didn't arise for the first eighteen months because I'd given up, really. Then we were sitting in a pub and he raised it. We were in Dublin and he started talking to me about having children (he'd never had any). I said, "Oh,

I'll never have children, it's too late." He said, "God, you're like Ian Paisley, you make up your mind and you never change it." We laughed. I thought why should I be such a bigot, why not give it another go? I was thirty-eight. We started trying. I made all sorts of assumptions that it would be terribly hard to get pregnant. But we succeeded straight away and it was a bit of a shock. However, we were both terribly excited and happy. We'd already planned a big trip to Australia and New Zealand and as I was in the early stages of pregnancy we thought we'd go, because I could still fly.

'Unfortunately, the holiday was dreadful. I was quite nervous about the trip because we'd never spent more than a weekend together and we were off for a month. I also had my own agenda. Ian was a very "unaware" man about men and women's issues and I think I lectured him too much. I desperately wanted to tackle him on his sexism. Also, because he earned more than me and owned a house, we'd agreed I would leave my job, move cities and live with him (he was now divorced). These were big changes I was facing and I was pregnant and very, very scared. The shit really hit the fan in Australia. We rowed the whole time about men, women and sexism. I think I was being hard on him and he said it wasn't his idea of a holiday. When we got to New Zealand I went off in the camper van for a few days alone as I needed time to think.

'I drove off to a beautiful, remote wild part and was on a campsite in the middle of nowhere when I started bleeding. I knew it was a miscarriage straight away. It was night, mud was everywhere and there was no one in sight. I didn't know what to do, but I'd noticed a shop about a mile away from the campsite. Bleeding heavily, I walked to the shop through muddy, icy roads and banged and banged on the door.

Eventually, a very kind woman helped me and I phoned local doctors who talked me through it all. They said I could either drive two hours at night, through mud, to a hospital or go back to the van and get through the night. I went back and spent an extraordinary night bleeding like mad, wrapped in towels. I was mourning the treasure of my heart. I'd also phoned Ian, who was at a barbecue in the city I'd left him in, and he was devastated. Next day I drove, wrapped in blood-soaked towels, back to the city. I felt very close to the child I was losing although the cramps were terrible. It seemed bizarre and cruel that the countryside I drove through was extraordinarily beautiful. I got to the hospital with Ian and they confirmed the baby was dead. Within an hour I had a d. and c. and then was back outside on the pavement, wobbly and shaky. We got on worse than before and couldn't get close to each other. It was an appalling holiday and I ended up feeling completely suicidal. I don't think Ian could really understand the depths of despair I was feeling. Back home, we were still completely shocked about the miscarriage and I said I needed time alone. I was now forty. I took a couple of months to recover and think. Although I wasn't over the miscarriage, I listened when Ian came to see me and said we should try again and do it quickly. I still wanted a child, but I was still really shocked. But I felt it was absolutely my last chance. We'd spent so long building the relationship and I didn't feel I had time to start again with someone else. It was now or never.

'I thought it would take me ages to get pregnant at forty, but I got pregnant straight away. Again, we were excited and I think it brought us back together. We had another panic at eight weeks and I thought the baby was dead. Then we had a scan, and I saw a little rice crispie with a beating heart and felt incredible excitement. The baby was alive. I felt confident when I saw his heartbeat. Amazingly, from then on the pregnancy was completely normal, with no complications. The birth itself was horrendous - thirty-six hours long. I was determined not to have drugs, but I spent twenty-four hours screaming. I'm only size 8 in clothes, so I'm pretty slim. I couldn't push the baby out and they put me on a drip to speed up the contractions, but I still couldn't push him out. I had an emergency Caesarian in the end. Both Ian and my mother were completely traumatised and I was utterly exhausted. However, the baby - who was 8 lb. 6 oz. - was utterly fine. I was totally devoted to him from the second I saw him, as was Ian. We'd just moved in together and I think we were a bit on our best behaviour, being nice to each other. After all, we hadn't lived together before. But our relationship grew as we were drawn together by looking after Robin.

'I couldn't believe, after all I had been through, that at forty-one, I finally had a baby. A healthy, happy, relaxed baby at that. He was a calm, self-confident little boy from the start. All he really needed was warmth, love, milk, security and I was able to give him that. It was the most wonderful thing to finally have him in my arms. In fact, my health has been fine ever since. I now work part-time, but I know my child is the most important thing in my life. I decided only to have one and not try again as I wanted to have all the time in the world for him. I saw a lot of my friends having a second one very close in time to the first and really struggling. Of course, if I'd managed to have a baby in my thirties it might all be different, but I didn't.

'Naturally, being with a very boisterous, vibrant, healthy four-year-old boy is very tiring, but I feel perfectly able to look after him. Almost more so than the able-bodied women I know, because I am very relaxed about health issues due to what I've been through. I don't panic, I don't worry any more. I feel I've already experienced being old with ME and cancer, and now I'm having my second youth. I know how important living is, really enjoying life and living it to the full. I'm making up for lost time and I feel really able to live in the present these days. I don't worry about the future at all. I've got the all-clear on the cancer and I feel very positive about my life and my health. I don't have to prove myself in the world any more either, so I can fully enjoy life with my child. Ian's been a very active and devoted dad, too, even though Robin was born when he was forty-nine. Despite everything, I feel we have both been amazingly fortunate and I thank my lucky stars every single day.'

6

Myth 5: Only is Lonely

REALITY TODAY: LONE PARENTS
OVER FORTY ARE FINE

Being a lone parent used to be a thing of shame. Women who had babies alone were scarlet in hue and wholly unfortunate. Thirty years ago, there was an assumption that a woman having a child alone had either committed a 'sin' by having sex outside of marriage or had been unfortunate (or careless) enough to have been abandoned by a feckless man. Lone mothers were lonely, they were looked down upon and were definitely 'less than' their stolidly married counterparts. Widows, left to bring up children alone, were pitied and their lives were assumed to be over for ever.

Of course, bringing up a child alone is neither simple nor easy, especially if bereavement and/or infidelity is involved. However, the shameful social stigma surrounding lone parenthood in the past has been largely replaced by a far more positive, forgiving and healthy attitude today.

Celebrity Lone Parents

Highly publicised lone parents, like celebrity mothers, have either decided to 'go-it alone' or have made being a lone parent a success after relationship breakdown. This has helped reduce the stigma of lone parenthood.

Halle Berry	Sofia Vergara
Sandra Bullock	Christina Aguilera
Jerry Hall	Calista Flockhart
Meg Matthews	Mel B
Fergie	Heather Small
Meg Ryan	Patsy Kensit

In fact, due to relationship breakdown and divorce, it is possible to claim that lone parenthood is virtually the norm these days. With one in two marriages failing, women often find themselves looking after not only their own children but also their step-children from previous liaisons. Maintaining relationships with past partners and husbands, for the sake of the children, can make the present family situation and any future relationships extremely complicated. In the twenty-first century we are becoming used to the notion that few people have one partner for life and that being part of a family can mean a wide range of things, including lone parenthood.

Going it alone

Some women find themselves lone parents at forty plus due to marital breakdown, separating from their partner, or the death of their partner or spouse. But what about the women who have been single most of their adult lives, or who have had a series of relationships without having children? There has been a growing trend in recent years for women in this situation to decide, as their mid-thirties and then forties approach, to go it alone having a baby. The rapid ticking of the biological clock has a lot to do with this decision, along with the decrease in social stigma attached to being a lone parent. Plus, technology has developed to the point that a single woman can now be inseminated by donor sperm if she has enough money to pay for the treatment. Some women simply ask a good male friend to oblige by donating their sperm, or they may have a one-night stand without using contraception. The rule book concerning what constitutes a family has simply been thrown out. This means there is greater opportunity than ever before for forty plus women to have children, whether they have a life-partner or not. Of course, considering the welfare of the child is paramount and most women will think very long and hard about whether they have the emotional commitment, time, energy, money and support to provide for a child alone.

Accidental pregnancy over forty

Some women, getting pregnant by 'accident' over forty, may well decide on a termination, precisely because they feel they will not be able to provide all that a child needs. But for others, having an 'accident' may actually be a subconscious way of making sure they have a child before it is too late. Some people would argue there is no such thing as an accident over forty because, surely, someone of that age and experience doesn't really make that kind of mistake, at least, not consciously. We know the subconscious works in mysterious ways and, indeed, it was the driving force behind Petra's 'accidental' pregnancy.

Petra's story: accidental lone parenthood over forty

Petra, forty-five, lives in an elegant flat with her daughter, Sophie, who is now five. She works full-time as a community doctor and her daughter now goes to school. 'I thought I'd probably never have children,' explains Petra, 'it was something I thought I might do later, but I didn't really feel old enough somehow. I sort of thought I was younger than I was. When I turned thirty-eight I thought: I'm not thirty-eight, I'm twenty-eight. I think time passes while you're busy and you don't really notice it - and then suddenly, there you are, wham, a forty-year-old, and you don't really believe it. Anyway, I had no intention of having a child. I was retraining as a doctor and working very hard. I went on holiday to South America with a gang of friends and I met a bloke there and we used contraception (well, there was the odd time we didn't), and the upshot was I got pregnant. It was an "accident", although people do say there's no such thing as an accident at my age and I can see their point - especially as I was training to be a doctor.

'I'd always been very careful in my relationships before. I didn't usually fling myself into situations, so this was fairly crazy for me. I'd come to the end of a very long relationship and I was sure I didn't want children with my "ex", although he wanted them with me. Finding myself pregnant with a relative stranger was an absolute shock. I went through a lot of serious heart-searching. I thought: What am I going to do? and I considered abortion. I'd recently been through so much emotional upheaval that I thought, in the end, I would stick with the pregnancy. I thought perhaps I should have some connection with the father, and I wrote and told him.

'To my astonishment, he wanted to be involved. Coming from a poor country, he had no ability to support me financially and, emotionally, he couldn't really do much because he lived so far away. He eventually arrived in the UK four weeks before the baby was born - I paid his fare. At the time, I thought him being there at the end was important but, in retrospect, I'm not so sure as things have got very complicated. I also visited him a couple of times while I was pregnant.

'I was working long hours and studying for exams at the time but, nonetheless, I had a very trouble-free pregnancy. I think the doctors were concerned that she was a bit small, but I'm really small. I think because I am a doctor I didn't get too bothered about all the physical stuff; I felt in control. I was just forty. I think it's like most things in life, you just get on with it. But, emotionally, it was very hard. I began to think about the other relationship that I had ended and started having second thoughts about it. But I stuck to my guns and didn't contact him. I don't think he knows to this day about my daughter. I felt like I was in the breakers, like my feet had gone from underneath me, especially at the beginning. A bit of a mid-life crisis, I think - there I was, trying to sort out one situation, and along came another one - one with major complications. However, I think there were things about my own past that made me contemplate lone parenthood more easily than most.

'My mother brought me up on her own, so I knew it could be done - or maybe I thought that was how it *should* be done, I don't know, but I feel a bit as if I'm following a pattern. My own parents split up when I was young. My mother was Austrian, my father Italian. They came to the UK before the war. When they split up, my father went back to Italy and remarried. His current wife felt threatened by his first family, so didn't want us to meet. I never saw him again and have no idea if he is alive. A friend of mine is Italian and lives in France, and I sent her a letter to send on to him. She even rang him up on the phone and said he sounded a bit doddery. From what my mother told me when I was a child, my father sounded like he wasn't much committed from the beginning of their relationship. In the telling of it, I think Mum had made it sound like she was very fond of him and that she wanted a child, but that he was less interested. The last time I saw my father was when I was a young child. I don't remember it, but my mother told me, and even that is a blur now.

'I never saw my Austrian family, either. She was Jewish and she only had one distant relative over here, who's now dead. My mother was an only child, her father had died when she was young, and her mother was killed in Auschwitz. So there wasn't much family around, it was essentially me and my mum. We were not well-off and I remember being terribly embarrassed about my mum because she didn't wear high-heels and make-up, and her style was awful. I also remember being embarrassed because we didn't have enough money to have fitted carpets and nice things. Later, I was glad about that because she gave me a perspective about what really mattered. She died of heart problems, however, when I was twenty. She was fifty-four. This was a terrible blow, a major thing, especially as I'm an only child myself. She didn't go to synagogue and we didn't have any family here, so I felt detached from my roots. As a kid I always wanted a big family and lots of people around. I'm also conscious of this for my daughter. I think the time when kids separate themselves emotionally from their parents is very critical and important.

'Anyway it's one of the main things that made me get my daughter's father involved in her life - although I regret it now. I've made a rod for my own back. The pregnancy and birth were very straightforward, no complications at all. The biggest complication was having Sophie's dad here. Circumstances meant that he stayed and we married - or rather, we married so he could stay. I was quite worried about coping before he went back, I was prolonging it, postponing it. But when he was here with us, it was stressful for all sorts of reasons. There are relationships that support you and those that don't and ours was the latter kind.

'In retrospect, I think it would have been better for him not to have come at all, or just for six months. He made no financial contribution, so it was a strain on me. I think he's still very selfish, too selfish to know what love really is although he says he loves me. I don't think I really loved him either, but I was prepared to see how far it went, how far it could grow. But he was very destructive in the relationship and three years, ago, I ended it. Sophie was one and a half, so she didn't really know what was going on. But since then, she talks a lot about her father and wants to see him. She says her dad is wonderful and uses him against me in arguments. She misses him and says she doesn't have enough of him. I let her stay in contact because my own experience taught me how important that is, but it does make things tough for me, as we won't be getting back together. I'm wiser now.

'So I am a lone parent now, like my mum before me. I love my job and have a very good childminder when Sophie's not at school. I never thought I would be a lone parent in my forties, but actually, I do pretty well. You have to compromise a lot to have a child - especially on your own - but that's OK.

'If this was my youth, I might feel resentful about not going out. I think I'm probably more calm about it all, more relaxed. I suppose a lot of that comes from my own mother, and a lot from life experience. If I were younger, I wouldn't have been through medical training, for instance, and that has given me a lot of confidence. I don't worry too much if Sophie gets sick. If she has a tummy ache, I say, "Sit on the toilet and let's see if something comes out." The knowledge I have gives me power in times of difficulty.

'Of course, I have wondered about having another child and I think it would be nice for her to have a sibling. But I am forty-five and I can't see it happening. I felt some pressure growing up as an only child, especially only having one other person in my family, my mum. When she went I lost everything and I do worry about that. I was involved in a car crash on the way home from work when Sophie was two and I broke a few ribs. I had to go to hospital, and couldn't pick her up from the childminder. That brought it home to me how tough it can be to be a single mum. I phoned a friend and got them to pick her up, and then I discharged myself and went home in a cab. I refused staying in overnight although the hospital wanted me to, because I simply couldn't: life had to go on. I suppose I've got used to having limits in my life.

'The problems in the relationship with Sophie's father have lingered on, so I've felt quite sapped by it in terms of finding someone else. And time has flown. I can't believe Sophie is five already, with her great long legs and all that. That's a bit shocking in terms of having another child - it would seem quite hard to start all that babyhood stuff again. I work five days a week and I don't miss Sophie when I'm not with her. Other people say they miss their children, but generally, I don't. I'm happy to leave her and I have been lucky with good childminders and a good nursery. I've had confidence in the places I've sent her. In the beginning, her dad helped out and that was fine. But in the end, it's been easier to do it alone, so as not to have to deal with him and all his stuff. Of course, sometimes there's pressure between work and her being ill and a partner would be good to have around. To be honest, I've packed her off with a temperature, having given her Calpol and thought: They can phone me if there's a problem. That's what can happen if there's no partner to juggle things with. However, I have developed swaps with other women because if she didn't have someone to play with at the weekend she'd go bonkers.

'The hardest problem is meeting my own needs. I don't think I meet them enough. Regarding my medical exams, it was very hard to get blocks of time to study when I needed to. I had to swot each night until 11 p.m. or midnight, after a full day's work and putting Sophie to bed. It was months of sheer grind to pass. I might have considered an au pair, but my flat is small and my income is limited. Another pair of hands would help a lot. I seldom go out of an evening. I think it almost takes too much energy to arrange it, and I don't have any energy left to do it. I usually share babysitting, if I do go out, and leave her with friends, as I couldn't really afford a babysitter. After a day's work and an evening with Sophie and bedtime, I'm usually quite happy to settle down myself for a good night's sleep, if I can. That's my biggest priority. I need to look after myself, otherwise things would fall apart. I've wondered what I would say to her if she said, "Mummy, why are you so old?" - I think I'd probably say, "Well, that's how I am, and you're lucky you got me. It's not what you look like, but how you are as a person, that counts." I'd probably come out with some old rubbish like that and we'd have a good laugh.'

Getting one in before closing time

Some women, like Petra, might admit to making a so-called mistake and have an 'accidental' baby in response to the booming of the biological clock or other emotional and physical pressures. If it seems very difficult to make a conscious decision, it can seem easier to let the subconscious do the deciding. 'Forgetting' contraception or getting sloppy about taking precautions can be a way of relinquishing responsibility about something which obviously seems life-changing and daunting - that is, having a child in midlife. Indeed, we're only human after all. It just might seem easier for pregnancy to come along after a one-night stand or holiday fling, than to agonise over it for months on end. Part of the problem for women who have been single for a long time or have put their career first, or who simply have not found a Mr Right, is what the hell to do when they want a baby without all the relationship paraphernalia thrown in. Some women will cold-bloodedly pick a 'stud' to sire their baby, others will ignore a man's failings and don't even need to be vaguely in love, because they so desperately want to have a child. So a stranger on a one-night stand will do. Women (especially professional women) have become so used to being in control, that when they want to have a baby, they often simply make an executive decision and then implement it, like a board-meeting agenda item.

The problem is that life, conception and having babies is hugely unpredictable and messy stuff. Keeping this in mind, it can be possible to make a decision to try to 'get one in before closing time' as I call trying to beat the biological clock before its last few bongs ring out, but there is obviously no guarantee that a woman will succeed. All she can do is listen to what her inner voice and her raging hormones tell her, make a decision and follow it to its logical conclusion. This is exactly what Carolyn did when she discovered she wanted to throw caution to the wind and try to have a child at forty-six - even on her own.

Carolyn's story: getting one in before closing time

Carolyn is now forty-nine, and works as a corporate fundraiser and PR manager for a women's health charity. She works full-time, just as she always has. The only difference is that she has a two-year-old child who goes to nursery three days a week, and is minded by her eighty-year-old mother for the other two days.

'I'd always wanted children, but had never been in a relationship where it was possible for me to have one. I'd actually got married at twenty-three, but it didn't work out at all. We were married for only a year, but it really put me off relationships. He was awful and it was the most dramatic year of my young life. After that, I think I put career first and got on with living and earning.

'However, when I got to my early forties I had a mid-life crisis. I was made redundant and my beloved father died within a short space of time. I entered a period of reassessment. What was my life about? Had I done all I wanted to? No, I still wanted a baby. So I went and got my fertility checked out as I had never got pregnant, and had no idea if I was OK or not. I discovered that my ovaries were bubbling away and everything was working perfectly normally. I started talking about having a baby with my close friends, my family, my eighty-year-old mother and her friends. I asked them, "If I had a child, would you help me bring it up?" I had a great response from them all. One of my friends had fostered children and she said "of course" straight away. I think I was on the rebound from my father's death and if I'd been more practical, I probably wouldn't have done it. But I felt time was running out. I had to think carefully. At the time, I was freelancing and it wasn't a very stable job. I really wanted to try for a baby, although I wasn't in a relationship, and I knew I could cope emotionally if I had loads of support from family and friends. I had a date with someone and didn't use contraception (typically, he didn't check it out or use it either) and I got pregnant at forty-four. I never told him, but I miscarried at seven weeks. I was upset, but at least I knew I could get pregnant. I had now got a full-time job at the charity, which was also an improvement in my situation. I knew the statistics about my chances of carrying a baby to term at my age were very low. And I knew one in three pregnancies ended in miscarriage so, to be honest, I knew it was all a very long shot indeed.

'However, eighteen months later, after another one night stand after a few drinks, though this time with someone I knew quite well, I got pregnant again. This time I felt very different in my body, it felt a much quieter, more solid feeling. I told my family and friends and I had amazingly positive reactions, they were lovely and very thrilled. However, I didn't tell anybody who the father was and I didn't tell him I was pregnant, either. I didn't want the complications.

'I had an amniocentesis at twelve weeks because there was no way that I could cope with a handicapped child. I knew how far my resources would stretch and that wasn't on. However, the results of the amnio were fine and I felt then I could relax. I started wearing loose clothes (I'd had to tell my boss two days before the test because I had to have time off to recover afterwards. She was supportive, too). One interesting thing to note about people's reactions was that while the women were supportive, the men went bananas. They would say to me, "You must tell the father, he has a right to know," and all that jazz. I felt I didn't want to cope with anyone else while I was pregnant. It might have been selfish, but I felt very fragile. Anyway, if a man doesn't want to be involved with a pregnancy, shouldn't he make sure he uses contraception? It takes two to tango, after all. Getting pregnant had been a real fluke for me. I'd used the Pill right up until my mid-thirties when I was advised to stop. My sex life wasn't that exciting. So I saw myself as being amazingly lucky at the time. I was forty-six, going on forty-seven.

'Anyway, the pregnancy was relatively problem-free - *at first*. I got swollen ankles at twenty-four weeks and the doctors began to worry it was pre-eclampsia. I was at UCH [University College Hospital] in London, which was excellent. It was actually the hospital I myself was born in all those years ago. I was monitored up to twenty-eight weeks for pre-eclampsia, but then my swollen ankles got better.

'I was under a consultant called Mr Silverstone, who was absolutely wonderful. He was positive, reassuring and kind. He never made me feel there was anything wrong about me going it alone at my age. He just said "What a triumph" and he meant it. That was very encouraging indeed. However, at twenty-nine weeks, I had to have bed rest as the pre-eclampsia was back, and worsening. They needed to monitor me closely and it wasn't clear the pregnancy was going to last. It was utterly devastating at the time. They took me into hospital and they said the baby was a threat to my life and I was a threat to her life because of the pre-eclampsia. It was dreadful. I stayed in bed, but by thirty weeks they said they had to do an emergency Caesarian otherwise we both would die. She was only 2 lb. 3½ oz. when she was born and she was put straight into an incubator. I didn't see her for twenty-four hours because they couldn't get her liver or kidneys functioning properly. I was also seriously ill and I found out afterwards that a lot of women die from pre-eclampsia, not just over forty, but young, too. It's a dreadful condition which women seem to get at the last moment, just before they are due.

'Eliza spent seven weeks in intensive care and I was there for two days after the birth. I had masses of milk and we tried really hard to breastfeed her, but it just didn't work. A baby's sucking motion doesn't start until thirty-two weeks, so she was just too young. I was heartbroken as I hadn't understood all the implications of her being a premature baby. I spent ten days in hospital and the staff were absolutely wonderful. The nurses taught me a lot and gave me loads of confidence in terms of looking after her. I hadn't really got a clue. The worst part was having to go home and leave little Eliza behind. I felt all the time that if I was there by her side she would survive, and I feared what would happen if I left. I remember she clung on to my little finger at five days old and looked up at me as if to say, "I know you're there, Mum", and I knew then she'd make it. Once I'd gone home I would go back every day and spend whole weekends in the special care unit just looking after my baby: touching, bathing, singing and talking to her. She was still being fed by tube. I willed her to make it and I saw what a feisty little determined thing she was - she really wanted to live. I loved her straight away and have always loved her since.

'Seven weeks later she came home with me - which was a wonderful moment. I had no idea what to do, although the nurses had been great and taught me a lot. I just got on with it. You just do. I had never got to a single antenatal class because I was too busy at work. I loved her from the start and the love spurred me on to do what was necessary. She's turned out to be a very healthy child with amazing hearing and eyesight. I thought she'd end up being sickly, but she's got an amazing energy and thirst for life.

'Then, when Eliza was a year and ten months, I started the menopause. I had really hot flushes and I thought it was a virus at first. I felt very tired and hot at night and it went on and off all the time. I then realised the flushes were happening every hour. I went for a blood test and found out I wasn't even pre-menopausal, I was dead in the middle of the menopause. There hadn't been any warning signs at all - just bam, there it was. I talked to my mum and she said she'd been fifty-one when she had hers; I was forty-nine, which I felt was a bit early. I wondered if it had something to do with the pregnancy, but discovered there are no rules, really - when it happens, it just happens, and that's it. Anyway, I went on HRT and within ten days my whole life had changed for the better. My maternal dementia disappeared, my nails grew back. HRT works for me, which I'm really glad about. I thought nothing was going to touch having those hot flushes, but the hormone patches and pills have worked very well. Of course, I felt sad that another baby would not be possible after this and that is a big regret. I obviously couldn't have another one now, not only because of the menopause, but because of my health and finances. Plus, the birth was very traumatic and I wouldn't want to go through that again.

'I told Eliza's daddy once she was born and he has become involved with her since, although we remain just good friends. Our relationship was always based more on friendship anyway, but he has been delighted with his special gift. Eliza knows she has a daddy, and that is important to me, although I live alone with Eliza. She has met his family, but they understand it's more of a friendship than a going concern. They are happy to have photos of Eliza and see her from time to time with her dad. He's been quite generous, putting money towards childcare and helping with buying the baby gear. I also had help from women friends - two of whom bought me the buggy, others gave me a cot and Moses basket.

'My friends have been very generous and really wonderful. But I think women have been the mainstay support in my life. I come from a long line of women who live to ripe old ages. My grandmother lived to a hundred, and died the year before Eliza was born. Her daughter, my mother, is an amazing eighty, so I think there's longevity genes on that side of the family. Anyway, in my generation, women in their fifties look a hell of a lot younger today than their mums did. In my mother's time, there were thirty-year-olds who looked fifty - today it's the reverse. It's not important what a mother looks like, it's more the patience, understanding and sheer enjoyment she can bring to the job. Eliza has brought me all the things I wanted all my life, so I'm only too pleased to spend time with her. I actually had a very happy childhood myself and enjoyed a good relationship with my parents and brother (and still do). He married late and had a child late, so my mother became a grandmother for the first time at seventy-eight.

'I'm sad Eliza won't be having a brother or sister - all children would like that I'm sure, just as I loved having my brother around. But she is surrounded by people of all ages nearly all the time. She already has some great friends and networks and it doesn't matter what their ages are. She either goes to two-year-old or eighty-year-old tea parties, which makes me laugh. She doesn't seem to care how old or young anyone is, they're just people to her. I also organise holidays and trips with loads of people. Last year we had a holiday with my mother, Eliza's father and loads of friends. It was a riot. I have loads of women friends who have had babies late, too, either with partners or without, so I include them in our weekends away or parties at home. She knows her cousin well and my brother and sister-in-law. I feel she has a real, extended family network all around her with lots of fun. It's nothing like the dour image people have of what it's like to be a single mum.

'I have to say, my daughter is the whole world to me. I feel being older has made me more assertive and confident, so she didn't have her MMR [mumps, measles, rubella] in one jab, for instance. I've researched the alternatives and have insisted each injection will be done separately. I'll pay for it if necessary or go privately. I think confidence comes with age. I know people say older mothers are overprotective and stifling, but she has so many people who enjoy her company and who share her life, I don't think that will happen with her. My most precious time of day is when I pick her up either from my mother's or nursery. We have a lovely chat in the car and I feel very close to her at these times.

'The hardest thing is the tiredness and lack of energy. But then I find I do have mental energy because I'm used to being exhausted in a work environment and pushing through it. I don't resent the fact that my social life is curbed at all. I've lived a lot of my life doing what I want, so I don't miss going out at night. I've done all that stuff. I might resent it if I were younger, but right now I don't feel I'm missing out on anything. I think you have to accept what life gives you - some women have their babies very young, some can't have any at all. I had mine this way round, late, and at least I know I've done a lot of what I wanted to and my child is really, really wanted. I don't worry about the future or being alone when I'm older. When she leaves home I'll be about sixty-nine and I'll just go back to watching the soaps with my feet up on the sofa. I think it'll be time for a good lie down.'

7

Myth 6: No Baby at Over Forty, No Children in Your Life

REALITY TODAY: YOU CAN HAVE CHILDREN IN YOUR LIFE AT OVER FORTY WITHOUT GIVING BIRTH

Women over forty who don't want a baby

At one time, the word 'childless' denoted a woman to be pitied. 'Childless' meant that a woman was incomplete, useless, not important in her own right. How times have changed. Over the past thirty years, as having children has become a real choice, many women have decided to live without procreating. As women's lives, opportunities and abilities have flourished, having children has ceased to be their sole *raison d'etre*. This cultural shift has meant women who have chosen not to have children are no longer thought of as weird or sad. It is generally understood they have made a choice. 'I'm perfectly happy not to have had children,' one forty-eight-year-old said to me, 'because I have plenty of children in my life through family and friends.' Of course, not being able to have a baby - for whatever reasons - is completely different from not wanting a baby in the first place. Some women may not actually like children or may have been put off having babies by their family history or personal experience.

Joan Smith, forty-six,
Author and Newspaper Columnist

'Children have never interested me. I don't think, "Gosh, they're sweet." As an only child, I was used to the company of adults and always happy to play by myself. I grew up on council estates and watched women who weren't much older than children themselves, having babies. Their lives and choices were restricted before they had ever begun... I'm always surprised by the assumption that everyone wants children. Child rearing requires a certain set of interests and skills which not everyone has... I cherish my independence. I have boyfriends but I don't want to live with anyone at the moment. My passion is writing. I have written five novels and five other books; it gives me immense satisfaction. There is something wonderful about being in your forties without children. You have a huge range of options. I go out dancing and travel as much as I like. I have friends who are older than me and still stay out into the early hours. If I want to I can live like a teenager... one night [in Malta recently], the bar closed at 11 p.m. so we caught a bus and hopped from club to club. No one thought we were odd. A woman in her sixties in a leather mini skirt was dancing on the table. Age simply wasn't an issue.'

From 'Why I'm Glad I'll Never Have Kids' by Sarah Dunn, in *Red* magazine, February 2000

Apart from those not wanting children at all, other women might not have found the right partner and may feel quite ambivalent about motherhood: 'If it happens, it happens, but I'm not that bothered if it doesn't,' one woman said to me. Some women may be bisexual or lesbian and although it is not impossible for gay couples to have their own babies via artificial insemination, surrogacy, fostering or adoption, it may simply not suit their lifestyle or relationship. Some women might simply have put their careers first, thinking, 'I'll have one later', and later never comes.

Abortion over forty

Some women who get pregnant over forty 'accidentally' may then decide (for whatever reason) not to continue with the pregnancy. Maybe the family are all grown up, and a couple simply cannot face nappies all over again; or maybe a woman is single and fears the loss of pension and promotion. It may simply be that she feels she cannot cope with pregnancy over forty - physically, emotionally and financially. There are as many women having abortions over the age of fifty as under sixteen (about seventy to eighty a year), which means many women clearly decide not to go ahead with late pregnancies due to their situation in life and/or age, according to Julia Berryman, ex-Senior Researcher at the Parenthood Research Group at the University of Leicester.

While there are so many women desperate to have a baby forty plus, it could seem very unfair that some women seem to get pregnant so easily over forty. Perhaps this underlines just how individual a thing fertility is. Deciding to abort a baby is never an easy option at any age, especially when it might be a woman's last chance of procreating. *Woman's Journal* carried a heart-rending article by writer Clare Allen which gives an insight into the agony of deciding to abort over forty. I quote it at length here because it is such a poignant and vivid account of what many women must have to go through in relative isolation.

Clare's story: having an abortion over forty

'I shouldn't have been surprised to find that I was pregnant because I had been a touch careless, and from experience I knew that I could fall pregnant at the drop of a hat - or cap. I was forty. My son and daughter were at school and we hadn't had a nappy in the house for some years. There was a dusty potty at the back of the airing cupboard, but otherwise all the baby-related stuff seemed a thing of the past. I didn't *know* I was pregnant at this stage. My period was just a few days late, but my mind was spinning.

'On Sunday my husband, Simon, said, rather surprisingly, "Isn't it time you had a period?" "Probably," I said guiltily, "it's a day or two late." He looked gloomy. "Don't worry," I added. He worried. The next evening, I said to him defensively, "And if I am pregnant?" He said I had to have an abortion, and if I didn't he'd leave me. I remember going completely cold and my hands started to shake. How could this man whom I loved so much, and who I thought loved me, be saying this? The part of me that wasn't frozen with misery was boiling with rage. What was all that old stuff about the woman's right to choose? I didn't know the Abortion Act had been passed to keep men happy. In retrospect, I don't think Simon would have left me if I had gone ahead with the pregnancy, though he was adamant at the time. He was panicking, as I was. Perhaps if I had had longer to come to terms with the idea of being pregnant, I would have been stronger. As it was, I didn't particularly feel I wanted another baby. But I didn't want an abortion either.

'By this time, a familiar feeling of exhaustion and nausea was telling me that the pregnancy testing kit I had bought had been no more than an academic exercise. Once, Simon rang me from work and said grimly, "OK, you win." But by the time he came home he had changed his mind again. A day later, I phoned him at work and told him for several long minutes that I thought he was a complete swine, without feeling or decency. I could hear him almost in tears in the office and I was pleased and spiteful.

'Like an automaton, I went along to a counselling service. I told them I had completed my family, that the financial burden of another baby would be too great and that I wanted an abortion. I resented the whole process. I hated the friendly 'help yourself' coffee in the waiting room and the right-on air of smug liberalism. Would I have welcomed all this if I had been a teenager? But here I was, middle-class, practically middle-aged and apparently in control of my destiny. I bridled at the thought of talking to some caring counsellor. But the rules say you have to do this, and I tried to act my way through the interview. I don't suppose she was convinced because I started crying when I asked her out of the blue if the embryo would... feel anything? She said that she didn't honestly know. The counsellor signed the forms, but invited me to come back and talk to her again. I never did, and I regret that too. She wasn't patronising and things might have been different if I'd talked a bit more, talked my way out of that reeling sense of panic.

'A few days later, I arrived bright and early at the abortion clinic, feeling about as bad as I've ever felt about anything. I was seven weeks pregnant. The nurses and administrators were very kind. I paid by credit card, got into bed and waited. I toyed with the idea of running away, and wondered how often someone hops out of bed and asks for a refund. When they came to get me with the trolley, it was as though I was being taken outside to be hanged. Just outside the operating room, I started to weep quietly and someone took my hand. Then, blissful unconsciousness. I woke on my way back to the ward with something like a mild period pain and a feeling of warm contentment. I was hungry and happy. I no longer felt sick. I felt enormously relieved. Had I done the right thing after. all?

'A couple of hours later, Simon came to pick me up. He looked terrified when he arrived and was pitifully relieved to see me in such good form. I waved to the nurses, bounced out of the clinic, chattering and cheerful. I think this may have simply been a hormonal high of some kind, for within forty-eight hours, I felt as though someone had slammed a brick in my face. I went to Tesco and the sight and sound of a very young baby paralysed me with grief. My misery shook Simon deeply, awakening his own feelings of guilt and regret. Sometimes we were kind to each other. Sometimes we hated each other. We went to Rome for the weekend. It was a disaster. I would wake in the morning and once again suddenly be conscious that I had had an abortion. It seemed to be written on the bedroom curtains in capital letters. My heart would begin to hammer. The thought of having done something irrevocable appalled me. I felt that my life had been utterly blighted. I couldn't think about anything else, and I began to feel so weary with thinking about this awful thing. One night Simon said he didn't think he could stand any more. I was crying as usual. And I just stopped there and then. I told myself I would never mention it to him again, I could say I stopped loving him at that moment, which would sound suitably dramatic, but it wouldn't be quite true. I do love him. But part of me is terribly angry with him for making me have the abortion. I am also angry with myself for letting anyone coerce me. But although I stopped talking about it, the abortion was the first thing I thought about when I woke up and the last thing I thought about at night. I have spent many hours crying in the bath. I felt stabs of jealousy whenever friends became pregnant - and an awful lot of them have. I wouldn't say I am "anti-abortion". For many women, it is absolutely the right decision. But it has to be *their* decision. I don't want to sound like a complete mad woman. Over the past two years I have taken pleasure in work, holidays, and the children's achievements. I have laughed and cooked and gardened. But I cannot forget this one, bloody awful thing I have done, which was a colossal mistake and caused me incalculable pain.'

Clare Allen's story is a powerful account of a woman feeling totally railroaded into making a decision before she was ready. Many women who have terminations over forty will do so because they know they just can't cope with having another child late and abortion is a so-called 'necessary evil'. However, I have spoken to several women, like Clare, who have felt immense pressure from the men in their lives, or from doctors, or society as a whole, to abort a perfectly viable baby purely because of their age. It is therefore essential that a woman gets the time - possibly also the counselling - and other emotional support that she needs to make a decision for herself in these circumstances, otherwise the mental anguish can scar for life.

Deciding on an abortion

Obviously, each woman has to weigh up her own circumstances and inner desires:

- If she already has children, what would the impact of a new baby be on their lives?
- If she is married or in a long-term partnership, either with or without children, could the relationship change at this late point to accommodate a baby?
- Are there any health or gynaecological problems which would make a pregnancy difficult? Can they be sorted out?
- Can the couple, or the woman, afford a baby? What will happen about childcare? Who will give up work or what are the alternatives if both of you want to continue working full-time?
- If the woman enjoys her career or job, how would having a baby affect her work, her promotional chances, her pension? If she is self-employed, can she afford it? Are there adequate maternity rights?
- Is the woman fit enough? Does she have any physical disabilities that need taking into account?
- Is the man fit enough? Would he be an involved or an absent father (crucial for a career woman or a disabled woman)?
- Do you *really* want the baby? Do you *both* want the child? If you do, are you both willing to work together to give the child what it needs - and that includes making personal sacrifices, such as time, career promotion, money, health, leisure activities, holidays, new cars, other luxuries.

Time needs to be spent thinking about these questions seriously. The answer may be obvious from the start: 'We can't possibly have this baby at this time of our lives', and the decision to abort may be relatively painless (although on a psychological level, it seldom is - women can still mourn the loss of their aborted children years after the event). For some women it is not a clear-cut decision.

Women who can't have a baby

Some women, like Clare above, may decide - albeit reluctantly - not to have a baby conceived after the age of forty. This may be a straightforward decision, or may be agonised over, as in Clare's case. However, there are many women who *can't* have a baby after forty, no matter how hard they try. In the bad old days women just had to accept their lot, and perhaps became doting aunts, if they were lucky. Today, there are many more options available to women, and we will explore them here. As families have opened their boundaries - and indeed, the very nature of family has changed - it is now perfectly possible for women over forty to have children in their lives without necessarily giving birth. Of course, there are women who very much want to have children and can't, either due to fertility or other physical problems, or because they haven't found Mr Right in time. I would not underestimate for a moment how painful it must be for a woman who really wants children not to be able to have them. And I doubt that having contact with other people's children would ever completely take away the ache of not having her own. However, women are now able to fill their lives with so many meaningful activities that the loss of not having a child can be ameliorated to a greater extent than ever before. There is also more counselling help available and we now acknowledge that people need to 'work things through' in order to process them. The spectre of a Miss Havisham, sitting in her decaying wedding dress, as in Dickens's novel *Great Expectations,* is a fearsome image of a woman's life wasted. Few women today will shelve themselves for life should they not be able either to have a baby or a relationship.

Of course, none of the options are that simple, and most will involve a considerable amount of time, planning, care, money and personal commitment. The point is that, as social rules have slackened and as we have got used to 'family' being created in all sorts of ways, it is entirely possible for a forty-plus woman to have children in her life today, even though she has not had a baby herself. We don't think lone parents are odd or shameful any more (see Myth 5, previous chapter). Equally, we don't look askance at an older woman (or a couple) being in charge of someone else's child on her (or their) own. Our perception of what women are capable of, and how relationships work, has changed, and thus many childless women - who like children and who want contact with them - can actually enjoy it today.

Significant relationship

An interested adult can be a real boon to any child, whether outside of the family or attached to it. If you are a woman who has not been able to have children - or have simply left it too late - and you want some kind of meaningful contact with a child, then this part of this book is aimed at you. Children need as much love, attention, validation and stimulation as they can get. Parents are often tired and caught up in everyday problems, like work, money, wider family demands such as caring for elderly relatives and their own relationship, so their children don't always get all the attention they need. An interested, caring adult who takes time to build a trusting and loving relationship can bring a lot not only to the child, but to the family as a whole. This can be a truly symbiotic relationship, in that the childless woman (or couple) can have a child in her (or their) life, and the family concerned can have an extra resource in caring for their child.

Abuse

Of course, it would be remiss of me to write a book advocating adults spend time with children not their own, and not mention the thorny issue of abuse. Child abuse has become an open sore in our culture. At least today we are able to talk about something which was brushed under the carpet and patently ignored thirty years ago. Any adult who knows they have or thinks they have been abused themselves (physically, sexually, emotionally) will need to think very carefully before they have contact with children. Some people deliberately avoid having their own children because they feel too hurt by their own past to contemplate being responsible for a child. Sometimes this is because they don't trust themselves to act appropriately. Or it may be because simply being in the presence of a child will bring up all sorts of difficult, painful and complicated feelings.

In some ways, abused people protect themselves from the past, psychologically, by not having children, and if this is true of you, you may well have made a very wise choice. If your husband or partner has been abused, it is something which needs airing thoroughly between you, or at least with a counsellor or GP, before you take on caring for or relating to a child. You both need to be clear that you are both trustworthy and that when difficult issues arise, you will be able to be honest about them, at least with each other.

Children's bodies are very open (think of all the nappy changing, rough play and nakedness) and uninhibited in how they dance and cavort. Any adult who feels they will find this difficult to cope with should seek professional help and certainly avoid having close contact with children, no matter what the addictive pull. (It is no coincidence that some adults who have been abused themselves can find themselves veering compulsively towards child-centred professions, like teaching, social work, childminding, etc.) However, if you or your partner have been abused, counselling and/or therapy can do a great deal to heal past emotional damage and there is no reason why, with time, effort and thoughtfulness, you should not go on to be perfectly adequate, safe and loving carers of children. This will not be true for everybody who has been abused as a child, of course, and a fine, honest judgement has to be taken concerning each person's ability to provide safe and loving care for a child.

Note to parents on abuse

Equally, any parent who entrusts their child to the care of someone in the family, a good friend, a close acquaintance or colleague, must think carefully before they do so. I don't mean to engender paranoia - there's enough in our culture today to drive all of us mad - but it is essential that parents take responsibility and check out the person concerned, not only in terms of seeing references if employment (for nannies, childminders, babysitters), adoption or fostering is involved, but also in terms of listening to any intuitive feelings they may have that there is something 'not right' about someone. Sometimes, it is hard to articulate exactly what it is about somebody that makes you feel uneasy about them being in the presence of children. Perhaps they are overfond of touching the children, or they are over-rough? Perhaps they believe in smacking or are punitive, or kiss or touch too much, have rigid rules, or play mind games in a way which makes you feel very uncomfortable? You may not even know exactly what it is that you are not sure of, but I would say trust your judgement.

Too many children have been manhandled (literally) because the adults who gave them over to someone else did not trust their own misgivings (as in the horrendous case of Victoria Climbié who was tortured and starved to death by her foster parents - all the obvious signals of abuse were ignored by professionals, relatives and neighbours). People fail to act on these obvious signals because any doubts seem to be too embarrassing or awkward to raise with the adults concerned. We still do tend to believe adults rather than children. If parents leave their child with somebody, they need to make sure that they are there during that person's first time together with their child. Parents should watch how the adult is with their child and observe how the child responds to them. I believe children intuitively know who is 'safe' and who isn't, and they tend to gravitate towards people who offer no threat. If they sense danger or violence, they may well not be happy with being left, and a parent should always pay attention to these feelings and allow them credibility. Better safe than sorry every time.

Working with children

Safety warnings aside, there are many opportunities for women to have significant contact with children if they have not been able to have their own children. Bessie, a forty-five-year-old nanny, told me, 'I had several miscarriages during my thirties when I tried to have children with my then husband. I think it was six, altogether, and it really broke my heart. It also broke up our relationship, which was foundering anyway. I was working as a PA in publishing at the time and I thought: "Well, if I can't have kids, I'll jolly well look after someone else's."' Bessie decided to do a nursery nurse training course at her local further education college, which she did part-time, before becoming a nanny at forty-one. 'I know it is an unusual step for a woman of my age, but I was really bored with my job, and I now work with two families doing a nanny share. I've made new friends, I'm studying for a psychology degree, and I've got really fit. I earn quite a lot, and I can take holidays and breaks more or less when I want. It's been a wonderful new beginning and I get so much from being with the children. It's wonderful to see them grow.' Of course, there is a danger of becoming over-involved with children that are not your own. 'I am aware I could get very attached, so I've told myself I'll only stay one or two years in each job. I love being with babies, so I think that's what I'll do.'

Of course, there are many other professions, such as teaching (nursery school, primary school), that women without their own children can retrain for. And there are voluntary activities, such as running playgroups and work crèches, organising child-centred events in your local community (playdays, day trips), volunteering with local state nurseries and schools as a classroom helper, running events for children's charities or being a hospital visitor to children's wards. If you have particular talents, such as singing, dancing, acting, you could get involved in local drama productions, school drama and music societies, or church activities (Sunday school, harvest festival, nativity plays), which involve children.

Godparents/paraparents

If you come from a family which is religious or you have a friend who is religious, you may well be asked to become a godparent when a child is born. Depending on the faith, and the parents' desires, a godparent can be a very significant person in a child's life. The job description is very much about offering moral guidance and emotional support. You may be a port in a storm should there be a family crisis. You can have the child to stay for holidays or be a provider of days out and fun, or just do some good old fashioned babysitting from time to time.

Mary, now forty-four and single, and who was raised Catholic and is a library worker, told me: 'I currently have six nephews and nieces. Both my brothers are married and have had three children each. I was unable to have children because first, I had years of endometriosis, and second, my husband died of a coronary at thirty-nine, before I could get pregnant. I haven't met anyone else and I don't think I would be able to have children with them now, if I did. So I spend a lot of time being an auntie and godmother, and I have to say it has been a wonderful extension to my life.' She's been on holiday alone with two or three of the children, she regularly has them to stay or goes to the park with them on a sunny afternoon. 'It's great to know I'm special to them, because of blood ties, and I spoil them rotten. It's fun for me to buy toys and clothes, something I can't do for my own child. But, I have to say it's also great to go home at the end of the day alone, knowing I'll have a good night's sleep.'

'Paraparenting'

As our society has become more secular, the number of Christian baptisms and christenings has gone down. This has meant that the number of people becoming traditional godparents has also dropped. We also live in a multicultural society where Jews, Hindus, Muslims and other religious and ethnic groups have their own ways of caring for children through extended family and friends.

However, new ideas and practices have evolved among people who would not necessarily adhere to any kind of religion. There is still a deeply felt need by some people to have a 'naming' ceremony of some sort. Many people make up their own ceremonies, and even though there is no direct relationship to a religion, it can be quite a spiritual event. This has led some new parents to want to appoint special adults as carers for their children, just in case something happens to them (a bit like a traditional godparent). Some people put this into formal terms, such as drawing up guardianship agreements, and this can be done through a solicitor. Some late parents are very aware that they must make financial and other provision for their child 'just in case' and will set up trust funds, take out life insurance and bonds, and amend their wills accordingly, when a baby is born.

'Paraparenting' is a new term applied to a significant adult who forms a deliberate relationship with a child with the consent of the parent or parents. For instance, if a woman is having a baby on her own after forty and has a best friend, she might ask her to be at the birth and be her 'support' person. She might also ask her friend to be the 'paraparent' - to be the one she can call on when the going gets tough to take the child for a night, or come and care for them when they get sick, or babysit on a regular basis, or even be part of family holidays. Some women come to the conclusion that paraparenting is best after trying to have babies, or when exploring other routes, such as adoption, fails.

Claudette's story: Paraparenting after forty

Jamaican-born Claudette has lived in Britain since she was ten and is now a university lecturer in education. She spent years working as a primary school teacher in inner city London and has a real love of children. However, she has been unable to have children herself and is now considering the options available to her in mid-life. 'I remember not wanting children when I was doing all the things I wanted to do,' she says honestly about her life in the 1970s and 1980s. 'I got pregnant at twenty-six and knew I didn't want a child with the person I was going out with at the time. I made my own decisions about my own body and I had an abortion. I didn't tell the man anything about it. I didn't think any more about it and went on the Pill like most women of my generation.

'However, it got to about 1987 – I was about thirty-three at the time - and I started wanting to have a baby. I wasn't in a relationship at the time, but I knew that, one day, I would definitely want to have a child. I had a well-woman check and discovered I was in big trouble inside. I had ovarian cysts, and they were all gammy and horrible, so I had to have an ovary and a fallopian tube removed. Then I had endometriosis and I began to think, "Uh oh, will I ever be able to have a child?" Everyone said to me, "Oh, it's fine, you'll get pregnant", but I wasn't so sure. At the time, I was teaching in primary school. I really love kids and my favourite age group is three to eight, they are out of all that wetness and into their own personality, before they get into that heavy pre-teen thing.

'I had a lot of painful periods and was checked again, only to find I had fibroids. Two great enormous ones. I found it very stressful with prolonged periods and lots of pain, with blood-spotting in between. So I had an operation to remove them. I got fed up with doctors and hospitals, so I went to a herbalist, who was excellent. She was almost like a counsellor and told me to stop eating wheat, and look after myself better.

'By then I had moved into an advisory role in school. I was in a relationship and at the age of thirty-seven a miracle happened and I got pregnant. That was after I'd been to the herbalist and she told me my hormones were out of synch. I thought that was great, that I'd done it. But I miscarried at three months. It was very hard. Everything came away at the time and I felt very sad. Particularly because I haven't managed to get pregnant since and now it doesn't look like I will. I don't have any regrets about my earlier abortion, although occasionally I think the child would be adult now, and wonder what they would be like. It was the right thing to do at the time and I wouldn't have been the person I am had I not done other things with my life. Then I became a university lecturer in education, which I love, and I've been studying for my PhD for some time - I'm trying to finish it at present.

'Anyway, I decided I wanted to try adoption through the local council. I saw an advert which said they were desperate for adoptive parents and I applied three years ago. I wanted to adopt because I do want a child in my life. I felt if I didn't adopt I would have missed an intimate emotional relationship which is very special with a child. I think you only have that kind of trusting, loving relationship with children, really. I have a lot to give and would love to experience being a mum. I've got time, experience, insight and confidence on my side as well. Over the years, being a teacher has taught me a lot about young people of all ages and I have considerable patience. I want more involvement with a child, more quality time, doing the ordinary things parents do. I have to say I started off all enthusiastic, but I have become incredibly disillusioned over time. The council have been utterly inefficient and I have been really outraged of late. I'm now in a steady relationship, although we don't live together. I'm planning to adopt on my own and the council have said they see no problem with that at all.

'I went back home for a visit to Jamaica last summer because my dad had just died there. I rang the council before I went and asked them if everything was OK, and what was the hold up? They had only offered me one child way back at the beginning, and the offer was withdrawn when she developed emotional problems. Since then, nothing had come my way. What made me cross, was that when I got back from my trip I had a letter saying they still hadn't received a "police check" form from my partner. I was terribly upset. I asked them why they hadn't told me this before I went, as I could have chased it up. They'd had months to do this and for a while, it even made me doubt my boyfriend. Even though he wouldn't be adopting, he would have contact with my child. Was there something I didn't know which was holding it all up? He told me there was absolutely no problem and I believed him. Indeed, he'd sent in the form and it turned out the council had actually lost it. They are so utterly inefficient, it's unbelievable. My partner is fifty and has a step-daughter in the Caribbean. I know it would affect our relationship for me to adopt, but it is what I want to do. We lead very different lifestyles, anyway; he tends to go out at 9 p.m. to music clubs, when I'm going to bed. I say to him: "No way am I going out now, I'm too tired." It would be impractical to adopt together and we're not proposing to.

'So I'm still waiting to hear back from the council. I wonder, do they really want anyone to actually adopt their children? I have to say that now I've turned forty-five I'm mentally beginning to retreat from the whole business. I felt excited at first, but now I'm really worn down. I'm not as energetic as I was at forty-two. I think by the end of this year I'll probably give up. A girlfriend in America said I should go there to adopt. I also popped into Barnardo's recently and they said they could fix me up in a few weeks with a child, but I feel it would complicate things as I'm still ostensibly on the list with my council. Anyway, I think now I'm cooling off the idea as it's been so terribly difficult to get anywhere. I wanted a black girl, around three years old - do you think it's that difficult to find one? I asked the council if my being a lone parent was a problem and they said absolutely not. So I've no idea what the problem is. I'm on the brink of giving up.

'I've thought about my alternatives. I have thought about what it means not to be a mother - biological or adoptive - and have decided that it doesn't really matter to me that much. I have my own life, which I enjoy. I don't feel my life is dependent upon having a child, although it would have been nice earlier, I suppose.

'Occasionally I get teased in Jamaica, and they say it's being cold in old England which is why I don't have children. I think more and more about old and cold than I do about being lonely, actually. I never want to be old and cold. I won't be in this country, I'll be back in Jamaica in my old age. Anyway, I have to finish my doctorate and I'm very determined about that. My ambition is to be travelling when I'm ninety with a rucksack on my back. It would be nice to have a child toddling along with me, but not essential. I have thought of fostering, but don't want the emotional seesaw of getting used to someone, giving them a lot, only for them to go. I'd rather be with someone long-term and get through all the struggles you need to, together over time.

'I'm lucky to have a mixture of friends with children and without. I have this friend across the river who is having a baby and we've made an agreement that I can get as involved as I like. It's the 'paraparent' idea. I'm not religious, although probably I'm quite spiritual. I'll be at the birth and will spend lots of time with her and her baby (she's a lone parent). I'm looking forward to getting very involved, and yet I'll still be able to be alone and do my own thing. I've also got loads of children in my life through my six brothers, nephews and nieces all over the place. My father kept adding another one and another one before he died; the last one was number six, not with my mother, I may add. I have two brothers I'm very close to and I'm a very involved aunt with their kids.

'My niece rang up last weekend and begged to come over and spend time with me. We had great fun and I think it's lovely to be accessible and have other people's children around. It works both ways, very well. I suppose I don't consider myself to be conventional. If my life had been mapped out traditionally, I might feel differently about not having a baby, but I don't. It hasn't worked out. That's how it is, I'm quite philosophical, really.'

Adoption

Adoption is an extremely fraught and difficult business in the UK, as Claudette's story illustrates. It gets worse the older a woman (or the adoptive parent) gets, and it is impossible to adopt a child legally after the age of forty-seven. Although rules about adoption have improved over the last few years, there were still 75,420 looked after children in England on 31 March 2018, according to the Department for Education. The problem is that there are so few babies for adoption. Women who get pregnant accidentally either opt for an abortion or to keep their children (as lone parenthood is less stigmatised today). The children available for adoption are often older, from very dysfunctional homes and/or have physical, learning or emotional difficulties. Plus, most local authorities have embraced a policy which says that black children should be placed with black families, white with white, and so on. This is obviously understandable from a cultural/racial viewpoint, but it does mean that there may be more children available for adoption from a particular ethnic group than parents to adopt them. Inevitably, there will be white people desperate to adopt, who are unable to find a child, and who are driven to find other, sometimes illegal or unorthodox, means of adopting.

Celebrities Who Have Adopted Children

It has become quite commonplace for celebrities to adopt children - often because they have more money available, or because their relationships are notoriously unstable due to an international lifestyle. Celebrities who have openly adopted children are:

- Viola Davis
- Hugh Jackman
- Katherine Heigl
- Charlize Theron
- Lenny Henry and Dawn French
- Sharon Stone
- Michelle Pfeiffer
- Calista Flockhart
- Joan Crawford

Sharon Stone, forty-two, On Her Adopted Son Roan

After several miscarriages, Sharon Stone adopted Roan when she was forty-two with her husband Phil Bronstein, a forty-seven-year-old newspaper executive. Sharon said of Roan: 'He's my wonderful, precious little Buddha. He eats like a champion, he sleeps peacefully and he's the apple of his daddy's eye ... now that I'm a married woman in my forties, I feel open to taking all kinds of directions, both personally and professionally ... you know the expression "life begins at forty"! You get to a certain point where you live your life as who you are - you care that you stood your ground and did the things that have value to you... it's the best thing I've ever done in my life.'

Hello! magazine, July 2000

Adoption from abroad

In a recent case in the US, black baby girl twins called Eiara and Keyara were sold on the Internet by their mother Trander Wecker, through Tina Johnson who runs an adoption agency (the Caring Heart Adoption Agency), first to one set of mixed-heritage parents (the Aliens) and then to a middle-aged British couple (the Kilshaws) for double the price. This case is an example of the way in which vulnerable, desperate, older parents can be manipulated, used and abused. Not only did both sets of parents get hurt, but the damage done to the children involved may only surface in years to come. It may be very difficult for them to trust or form relationships, and their 'sale' will always be an emotional burden for them to bear. At time of writing, their natural father has applied for custody of the children, and they have been returned to the States, to be fostered.

However, childless couples with money have been able to 'buy' children for years, as a means of getting round the age limits imposed by British adoption rules. South America, Eastern Europe and China have become places famous for doing deals with desperate Western parents. Needless to say, these routes are usually only available to educated, professional, middle-class parents who have money. A 'home study' is usually done through a local adoption agency, or the local authority, to verify the parents' suitability to adopt and to guarantee the safety of the child or children adopted. Journalist Judi Bevan told me how she and her husband, John Jay, ex-editor of the *Sunday Times*, went about adopting their Chinese baby daughter, Josephine Chun Eui, who is now four. This interview was conducted while Judi was on her exercise bike, keeping fit at home, which struck me as very 'typical' of forty-plus mums, who often use every minute of the day to keep themselves up to scratch.

Judi's story: the long road to a Chinese baby

'When John and I met we had both been married before and neither of us had children. I was forty-seven and John was ten years younger than me. During my first marriage I had a miscarriage at forty-three, then another one fifteen months later. Afterwards I tried fertility treatment. I decided on egg donation and there was a very lengthy wait for a donor. After my marriage ended I met John, but I was disillusioned about my ability to have a child.

'John and I started talking about adoption once we'd decided we really wanted to have a baby together. We knew more or less we would be too old to adopt in the UK, certainly we knew we wouldn't get a child under two, which is what we wanted. There's a great shortage of babies to adopt and huge amounts of children in care, whom nobody wants. We felt we really didn't have the expertise to cope with a child who had been through multiple placements, so we began to research where in the world we could adopt. China had the most clear-cut system, plus, there were all those abandoned baby girls.

'The Chinese had developed a "one-child" policy which, combined with the Confuscian tradition, meant that boys were more valuable than girls. The Chinese believe that girls are not much use to you in old age. There are three million baby girls abandoned in orphanages and children's institutions (many die or are killed deliberately). They have very little in the way of physical or other education, so they mostly come out subnormal. We knew these children were genuinely abandoned. We didn't want to adopt out of philanthropy, however, we wanted our own baby - and a healthy baby at that. Indeed, we found out that if you adopt one child from the Chinese, and want to adopt a second one, they will give you a special needs one for number two. It's their rule. The Chinese basically regard orphans as worthless.

'Josephine was found abandoned on a doorstep in a little village in Fu Yang country. All we know is that she was wrapped in a quilt and left outside with a packet of powdered milk and a 100 Yuan note. Adopting her was a fairly irksome process. We first had to be assessed here by UK authorities for an overseas adoption [the home study]. It was done through our local authority and we were turned down initially. They said we worked too hard, were too highly educated and middle-class. They said we would put pressure on the child to succeed. The people who assessed us had no idea what was happening to children in China. We appealed and won the right to be reassessed. We were eventually approved and they plucked a child's details out of a computer and we got some sketchy information about her. We just said "yes". We had to pay £3000 to our local authority to get permission, then £3000 to the orphanage. We didn't know what they would do with it, we hoped they'd build a fabulous new wing, but there are stories of directors driving around in sports cars. It has improved over the past five years, I have to say.

'She was seventeen months when we adopted her. We'd just seen a tiny passport-size photo, and a few details in Chinese which we had to have translated. The Chinese government has a special travel agency bringing couples from the US and UK. We flew to Beijing and were met by a guide who put us on a plane to Hang Jo, the capital of Dejang province. We also had to take £300 for a settlement visa. I'd been on holiday to China before, so I wasn't that thrown, and John is an historian, so he was fascinated.

'We both liked the Chinese, their humour and intelligence, although we know the recent past has been sad and their human rights record is not good. Anyway, another guide met us and took us to our hotel and said, "I'll come and get you to meet your baby tomorrow." We were settling in, somewhat jet-lagged, when there was a knock on the door and there was someone standing there with a baby. *Our baby.* She wasn't very happy to be handed over to total strangers and was in severe shock for three days. We obviously looked different, spoke differently, smelt differently. She'd been brought that very morning from the orphanage. We handed over the £3000 to the woman that brought her and she gave her a cuddle - with some real affection - and then left. I was stunned, also very relieved, that at last we'd got her. We'd signed the papers and she was ours. We took off her seven layers of clothes and she clung to us like a little Koala bear. She didn't eat, she still drank formula at seventeen months. She smiled, we fed her, and then she slept. It was amazing.

'Bonding with her took quite a long time. I felt extremely protective of her and on the third day I felt a stab of love. We'd had a practically sleepless night, we were both jet-lagged and I was fairly full of anxiety. I woke up and took her into bed with me. She turned round and started to play with a little card. She didn't play with toys - she was terrified of toys, which were alien and threatening, and a cuddly toy was terribly scary. But the way in which she concentrated her whole being on this little card was terribly touching. I looked at John and we both felt a huge surge of affection for her. It grew from there. Of course, there have been times when I've thought, "What have I done this for?" As she's got older, it has been very demanding at times. Sometimes you don't have the energy to feel love, because of constantly entertaining, feeding, being on call. I had had no previous experience of looking after children. I'm an only child myself, so playing in the park felt a bit difficult. But I've got used to it.

'A few weeks after we got home she became much more physical. She would fling herself on me and start kissing me passionately. She was very much a daddy's girl and she loved all the physical rough play and romping he did with her. She's now much more of a mummy's girl, probably because I gave up my full-time, high-powered job to be with her. Giving up my career was a big jolt to the system. I'd interviewed 323 captains of industry for the *Sunday Telegraph* Business Section, where I had a column, and now I was changing nappies and mopping up poo and sick. I went through a period of grief for the workplace, because I loved walking into the office, saying hallo, getting a coffee, going to my computer. I enjoyed the companionship I had there while doing work I really valued. I do miss it and I would like to go back part-time, not five days a week. But I've made new friends and have gone to playgroups and things. I started writing a book part-time and after nine months, had a nanny-share with someone else. Josephine now goes to a local Montessori nursery in the mornings. Luckily, we have a good babysitter next door.

'I'm now fifty-three, John's forty-three, and we're quite complementary as parents. I'm quite tolerant, but he pulls her up if she doesn't behave well. I have a lot of mental energy, even if my physical energy flags. She does need to be listened to and I have time for her. I'm not too protective because I know she's got to make her own mistakes, I try to give her a feeling of control over her life as kids have so little control over anything. She is a very gorgeous child and most people smile gooeyly when they meet her. Sometimes kids in the park will say, "You're not her real mum, you're not Chinese; where's her real mum?" And I simply say, "She's adopted," and they usually go away. She's asked me questions and I've answered them. When we saw Pingu's mum having a baby, she asked if she had grown in my tummy. I said, "You grew in another mummy's tummy in China, your first mummy. I'm your mummy now." I think she's convinced her mummy is dead, but she hasn't got upset, not yet. I think I bring a lot of experience to the job. I was a bit of a wild child in my twenties and I simply would have been too selfish to be a mum, I couldn't have coped at all. Being older, I've got more patience and a broader view of the world. I'm learning Chinese, as is Josephine. She has met other Chinese children around here, and both John and I love China, so we will make sure she understands all about her roots. We have compiled information about her village, we go to Chinese New Year in Chinatown, we've given her a Chinese middle name. She tells people proudly, "I was born in China, you know," although she's too young really to understand what that means. She thinks it's just fantastic to be Chinese.

"The battle to adopt Josephine brought John and I much closer, although the first year was very difficult. We don't get as much time together as we did before, and he is at work, whereas I've given it all up to stay at home. I used to feel resentful when she screamed, "Daddy, Daddy, Daddy", the minute he was home, as if I was just part of the furniture (which, in a way, I have become). I think adoptive children can try to drive a wedge between their parents because they need to feel very secure, and we have had to get wise to that and make sure we stay strong as a team. Some of my friends disapproved of our adoption and I lost one of my best, fairly 'prima donna' type, friends who was always in a crisis. She'd had kids and we used to go on holiday with her. But the minute I had Josephine she would phone up, insensitively, between six and eight in the evening, which she knew was bathtime. It was like she was competing for attention, like another child. I only met one other mother over forty - a forty-seven-year-old - and, of course, I didn't need an NCT group as I wasn't a biological mother. But gradually I've made friends with other mothers who are much younger than me, through Josephine. I'm a bit out of synch with my own generation, whose children have left home already and are in their twenties or thirties.

'We did wonder about trying to adopt another baby, and would have done it if I'd been five years younger. We would have had to move house because of space and I suppose I just wimped out. I can't take any credit for Josephine's genetic make-up, but she is a bright, lively, intelligent little girl. We can only put in environment and nurture and we have taken as much care as we can. We have a little cottage by the sea and we go there as often as we can. She loves our seaside home and she gets very excited when we go there. We adore her having so much fun and we want to give her as much stability and love as we possibly can. Of course, I would have loved to have had my own biological child. But now I've got Josephine she is simply my own daughter.'

Fostering

Fostering is another way for women who have not had their own children to have a significant relationship with young people. Fostering is nearly always short-term care, but requires a great deal of dedication, sensitivity and stability on the part of the foster parents. Foster parents may or may not already have their own biological children. However, most of the children to be fostered will have come from very unhappy and dysfunctional backgrounds and therefore only people with a great deal of emotional self-knowledge, strength and the ability to love and care for children regardless of the immediate pay-off, should think about this option. For more information about fostering, contact: The British Agencies for Adoption and Fostering.

Sponsoring and hosting

SPONSORING

Open most Sunday newspapers and there will be an advert to sponsor a child in a third world country, perhaps in Africa or South America. Many childless people find it an extremely rewarding thing to do. This can entail simply paying a certain sum of money every month towards the upkeep and education of a named disadvantaged child. Sometimes there are visits, of the sponsors to their country, or of the sponsored child to the sponsor's country.

Sponsorship can also happen in the UK and some people work with children's charities and become visitors to children's homes or sponsors of specific events for disadvantaged children.

Hosting

Hosting children has also become popular. Organisations such as Friends of Chernobyl's Children bring children over to the UK every year for a fully paid-up holiday. The charity usually pays the fares and the UK hosts pay for the child's food and upkeep. Many children visit families with children, but it is also possible for women or couples without their own children to become hosts. This kind of arrangement usually requires a commitment to host the child once a year for several years and to maintain contact with the child in between. Many people find this kind of arrangement extremely rewarding, and it is another, highly significant, option for non-biological parents who want to make a difference to a child's life. 'I saw an ad in a local paper and we've hosted a boy for the past five years,' said one forty-five-year-old woman friend. 'Working for the charity has been the most fulfilling thing I could do, instead of being a mum.'

Sponsoring and hosting can be a wonderful way of transferring some of the excess wealth from the West to children who really need it, by forming real and significant relationships. Sponsors and hosts can play an important part in a disadvantaged child's life. Although sponsoring and hosting are both done at a distance, they are nonetheless an important commitment which should be undertaken with an open heart and mind and the right reasons, rather than just an open chequebook. People need to think long and hard about their ability to commit to such a project. Out of sight should not mean out of mind.

Surrogacy

Surrogacy is where one woman has a baby on behalf of another and hands it over once the birth is over. It remains a highly controversial way of having a non-biological child. It is, however, often the last desperate resort of couples or women who can't have their own children. A Surrogacy Arrangements Bill was passed in 1984 after Kim Cotton became the UK's first surrogate mother. She set up an organisation, COTS, which has put surrogate mothers in touch with childless couples ever since.

Controversy has always dogged surrogacy as it is a highly complicated and emotionally fraught way of having a baby. Recently, the exchange of money between the commissioning parents and the surrogate mother has been curbed even further in law, making it difficult for surrogate mothers to earn a living from growing babies in their own bodies for other people. Before the recent changes, surrogate mothers could charge for 'expenses' which was a loose term covering any amount of money they could negotiate, which usually ran into thousands. Now, the expense has become extremely limited and has put off a lot of surrogate mothers from volunteering their services.

Of course, surrogacy is emotionally fraught because the biological mother has to hand over her baby to the couple. Sometimes, once she meets her baby, the surrogate mother does not want to do this. Sometimes the donor parents reject the babies which are produced for them. And sometimes the law and society looks askance if the couple are gay or lesbian. Surrogacy is a legal and emotional minefield and should be entered into extremely warily and, hopefully, with counselling support and legal advice. Most surrogacy arrangements are done through COTS, but very occasionally close friends, even family, will offer their services to help out a childless woman.

Diane Kingston Brown's unusual surrogacy arrangement was reported in *Woman's Realm* (12 December 2000) and is a good example of what a forty-plus mother can do, if she is extremely fortunate. 'Like many women, my biological clock had begun ticking in my thirties. I was a personnel officer in the RAF and was often posted overseas. My lifestyle meant that I couldn't sustain a relationship, let alone think about having a child. So at forty-three I changed careers and became a lecturer in Essex. It was there I met Simon. He was two years older and separated with two teenage daughters. Simon was my soulmate. After a year we moved in together. Marriage wasn't a priority, but I still wanted children. After six months of trying, I was referred to a fertility centre in London where I was offered IVF treatment. Eggs would be fertilised outside my body, using Simon's sperm, and implanted in my womb. There was a two-year waiting list and the only way to avoid this was to find a donor myself. I advertised in a magazine, but had no luck. I didn't feel I could ask my friends.

'Then one day when I was visiting my sister Rosemary, who has two daughters - Kirsty, then twenty-two, and Lauren, eighteen, and a son, Greg, I thought: Why not ask Kirsty and Lauren? I knew it was a big thing to ask but Rosemary was very supportive and said she'd put it to them. We decided to give the girls two weeks to make the decision. The wait was nerve-wracking. I'm very close to the girls and I didn't want them to do it out of guilt because they felt I was desperate.' Kirsty agreed to try to have a baby for Diane. No money would be involved in the arrangement, although Diane would pay for any medical costs relating to the egg donation. Technically, Diane would be great-aunt to the baby, and Kirsty its biological mother and cousin. Having had some counselling, they proceeded with the egg donation.

'Five of her [Kirsty's] eggs were removed and fertilised in a test-tube with Simon's sperm. I waited three days to find out if the eggs had been fertilised. Luckily they had, and three were placed in my womb. My chances of a successful implantation were slim and I had to prepare myself for failure, but two weeks later my pregnancy test was positive. Against all the odds I'd become pregnant. The pregnancy was awful. I felt sick, lost weight and had to rest a lot. To come this far and lose my child would be devastating. Rachel was born in June 1998, and weighed 6 lb. 11 oz. Kirsty helped us choose the name and I asked her to be godmother. When I first decided I wanted to have children, I knew I didn't want Rachel to grow up as an only child; that seemed a huge responsibility - especially if Simon or I became ill.

'At first, I thought Kirsty would donate her eggs again, but she'd reacted badly to the medication and didn't want to do it again. Although I was disappointed, I understood. But a few months later, after Rachel was born, Kirsty's sister Lauren said she was happy to donate her eggs if I wanted another child. I jumped for joy. It meant I wouldn't have to wait for a donor or advertise and that the children would be closely related. Again, I became pregnant first time, even though the chances of this happening are very rare. The risks were no greater the second time, but even so I still felt anxious.

'My son was born on 20 May. We asked Lauren to be godmother and she helped us choose his name - Brandon. Despite all the myths that exist about being an older mum, it's great. I have patience, a wealth of life experience and energy. I glow when people stop me in the street and say how much alike my babies are and how much they look like me. As soon as Rachel and Brandon are older I'll tell them about their origins and who their biological mothers are. People ask me why I'm so open about my story. I say I want people to be more aware of the processes involved, so that more egg donors come forward. There is almost a 45 per cent success rate with donor eggs and, as my story proves, it can be a very positive experience for everyone.'

8

Myth 7: It's Not Fair on Babies to Have Them at Over Forty

REALITY TODAY: BETTER LATE THAN NEVER

Annette Bening Has Four Children With Warren Beatty – she was forty-three when she had their youngest, Ella Corinne

'To have four kids nowadays is a lot if you're going to have any kind of career... but each time I became pregnant I was so happy that I couldn't have cared less about being an actress.'

American Beauty star quoted in *Hello!* magazine,
September 2000

'It's just not fair on the kids', is one of the major cries heard against late motherhood. When I was researching this book I uncovered so many myths about people's perceptions of older mums. Out of touch, lethargic, unfit, boring, incapable of conceiving, unsexy. The prejudice about age - and ageing women in particular - is a very tangible thing in our culture. It's almost a crime to get old. Yet, all of us do. We know that there are many cultures which revere and respect age. Ours is not one of them. We have some kind of erroneous belief that human beings stop being intelligent, creative, sexy, adventurous, loving and vibrant when a few grey hairs and wrinkles come along. Yet, the women I met while interviewing for this book were simply not true to their stereotyped picture. Perhaps it's the stereotype that's out of date.

Rover's Return

'I had my youngest son, Michael, at forty years old and he was a fiftieth birthday present to my husband. When Michael was born (he's now twelve) I already had four other boys ranging from ten to eighteen. I'd desperately wanted a daughter, so becoming pregnant again over forty was a last attempt for that much-wanted girl. I'd had a miscarriage the year before, so the urge for a baby was quite strong. My husband broke the news to our sons: "You know that you wanted a dog (to replace the one we'd recently lost after fourteen years), well, the bad news is that we're not having a dog, but the good news is we're having a baby, so you can take it for walks and call it Rover."'

From a letter received at *Home & Life* magazine, July 2000

Forest of myths surrounding late motherhood

One friend said that the 'forest of myths' surrounding late motherhood had actually put her off trying for years. And yet, once she started on the path towards trying to have a child herself, each tree in the forest began to quiver, bend, then fall. It's time for us to take a hatchet to these myths which cloud the issue of late motherhood. If a woman does not want to procreate, then fine. But if a woman has reached forty and wants to give it a go either for the first time or to complete her family, then why not offer all the support, encouragement and information possible so that she can make an informed choice? It is not certain that she will succeed, but there is always a chance. And as long as there is a chance, there's hope.

Michele Oborne: Fourth Child at Forty - a Whole New Turning Point

'I had my fourth child two years ago after a gap of seven years. My best friend, like almost everyone else I told, was speechless. A fourth child at forty! I hardly dared to tell her that, unlike our first three children, number four was, if not planned, then certainly not unplanned. I knew, of course, that a new baby would mean a lot more work and chaos at home, but I had juggled a full-time job in the City while my first three were tiny - so why should number four be a problem? 'Just a few months into my pregnancy, though, I realised what a turning point the new baby was destined to be. I had spent more than fifteen years working hard to build my career and, as a director, I was reaping the financial benefits. Yet, I wanted to treasure every moment of being with my last baby, so I realised that continuing with a full-time job would be impossible. I loved my work, I had been involved in big international projects, but at a high price: I worked long hours, which often spilled over into weekends and holidays. And the job had never been the same for me since I had started a family.

My meetings on overseas trips had become absurdly compressed so that I could keep the number of nights I spent away from home to the minimum - on one visit to Chile (twenty hours of flying each way) I did four meetings, two lunches and a dinner in less than twenty-four hours on the ground - so I could get back in time for my son's first day at school. The thin blue line in the pregnancy test seemed to be drawing a line in the sand for me. I realised that, in the end, I could have it all but, if I wanted to start enjoying some of the things I was doing, then I would have to make a choice. I am very grateful for my fourth baby. Without her, I wonder whether I would still be hurtling through life at breakneck speed - ostensibly achieving so much, but in reality enjoying little. Now, having given up my job, I have found the time to write a novel, Mother Love, (Piatkus) about Louise, a mother of three who has a big job and also a

Continued

demanding family... Although as a family we have less money, only one car and no nanny, I do, at last, have much more time for the things that are really important in life - my children and my husband. And myself. I take great pleasure from the emptiness of my diary, I pride myself on having time to go for a walk and stop and chat with a neighbour, to read a book or write a letter to a friend. And this makes me feel far richer than I ever was before.'

From 'Come In Number Four' by Deborah Hutton, *You* Magazine, 13 August 2000

Keep hope alive

Many of the women I interviewed had given up hope, only to get pregnant once they tried in earnest or got the help they needed. Some felt they would never find the right man, until he suddenly appeared - after their fortieth birthday. Perhaps it is a salutary lesson for us in the twenty-first century that we don't, and can't, know everything. Even about our own lives.

I heard about far more women than I could possibly interview for this book. Each time I interviewed a woman she would say, 'Oh, I have a friend, and she has a friend, and I know someone else...' and so it would go on. I still have a list of twenty more women, dotted all over the country, whom I could interview. But I am not an academic researcher, nor do I have the time and money to do so. Rather, I wanted to write a book that provided an insight into what it is like to launch yourself into the unknown and against all the prejudices that abound about what a woman should be up to at forty plus today.

To some extent each of us is the author of our own life story. My own story, told at length at the beginning of this book, was a sort of shock for me to read back to myself. I had decided not to have children at five, had had huge physical and emotional problems to overcome, was nearly sterilised in my twenties, and yet, in my forties met the right man at last. It was a constellation of the right circumstances: the right man, at the right time, in the right place. I had written myself off as a mother. Yet, now, as a mother, I am so damned glad it happened, so grateful every day that I had the chance to have a completely wonderful child in my life. She is my little moon and star and I sometimes wonder how my life would have turned out without her. Yes, I would have carried on writing books and articles, I would have travelled and broadcast, had fun with friends and family, drunk champagne and gardened. Life would have been good. But, through having a child late, life has been more than good, rich beyond my wildest possible dreams.

This may be hard to read if you have lost children, decided against them, dislike them intensely or are wary of embarking on the path to IVF, surrogacy or adoption, or simply haven't had the chance to have a child. But I can only write what I feel and believe in this book - and that is that having a child, for me, was a major factor in healing my past hurts and in finally growing up. Not that I'm entirely there yet. Not that there aren't moments when I feel exhausted and overwhelmed, or frustrated or sad that I can't have another. But I have to say that I feel truly blessed.

This sounds fanciful and romantic, I am sure. But to those mothers who have succeeded in having babies at over forty, by fair means or foul, I am sure I make sense. And to the mothers who are wondering whether they will or should, I can only encourage. Try it and see. Why not try to get one in before closing time? I truly believe that it has been better to have had my child late than never. She may well ask me as she grows why I'm so wrinkly around the eyes or baggy about the bum. She may well fear my death, or be embarrassed by my age in front of teenage friends and boyfriends. So be it. I can only be myself, only bring her love and my best care - part of which is to be true to myself and also to her, whatever, and however she reacts. I feel confident enough to make a joke and tell the truth; I feel constant enough to be able to listen to her criticisms and not to take them personally; I feel big enough to love her while she hates me. I will be there, as her mum, throughout her life and of course, after my life, in her heart. I have worked hard to be there as much as I can - not only physically, but emotionally. So many of the older mothers I spoke to had the same refrain; 'I haven't had this child late in life not to be there for her.' Although I have worked - mostly part-time - I have made the effort to be there at those special moments: first steps, first dental and doctor visits, immunisations, Christmas and birthday parties, family events and just hanging out with her bouncing on the sofa, giggling.

This is not to say I am a perfect mum, how could I be? But it is to say that I have taken pleasure in the small every day moments, like picking her up from nursery and walking home chatting, which are like gold dust to me. And seeing her succeed through her teens and now early twenties has been extraordinarily rich. The years stretching out ahead look very different to me now – looking back, the summers were peppered with bucket and spade holidays; Christmases were wonderful, glittering with presents and stockings, trees and Santa Claus. I indulged myself to the full and enjoyed her childhood and my adulthood at the same time. Instead of going into a mid-life decline, I feel very fortunate to have had such a wonderful, meaningful project for the past twenty years running alongside my own career, life, and relationships.

Wait, you may say, but what about the child? Indeed, we may not know for some time whether older mothers are a curse or a blessing, but most of the research shows, so far, that the children emerge with solid social skills, confidence and a sense of self-worth. That surely can't be bad. The main issue is combatting the ageist prejudice which may make late children look askance at their own mothers over time. All older mothers can do is get wise to that fact and combat ageism at every turn by living out their lives as well and as honestly as they can.

Nearly all the women I spoke to for this book left me feeling uplifted and inspired, even when their stories contained pain and loss. I feel I would like anyone who reads this book to come away feeling warmed, encouraged and amazed at the power of the human spirit to overcome difficulty and the inexorable march of time. I would also love any woman who is hovering on the brink to feel she has a right to try, at least, to have a baby at over forty.

This is a final, inspiring story from Margaret, now sixty-one, who lives in Belfast and who contacted me through *Home & Life*:

Margaret's story: three sons after forty - certainly worth all the effort

'I didn't have sex until I was thirty-six, which seems amazing for these days. I simply didn't meet the right man until then, and that's a fact. I had worked as a civil servant from the age of seventeen to twenty-five and lived in London. I never really met the right man over there - I fell in love a couple of times, but it didn't work out. I began to feel a bit unsettled and came home again, continuing to work as a civil servant. I felt a bit odd when my friends got married. I had a strong maternal instinct, I really loved children, and I thought: Why aren't I getting married? What's wrong with me? I did grieve over it a few times. I come from a large family, I'm one of seven. There was one dead baby, too. I was the second eldest, with an elder brother above me. My parents were very happy together and had a very good married life. Their marriage was a good model to me and I felt very secure with them. My father died seventeen years ago and that was very, very sad. My mother died this year of Alzheimer's disease and it was a long, slow process waiting for her to die, which was very gruelling.

'I think I'd always had a mental blueprint of what I'd like in a man - intelligent, same views on politics and religion, a strong spiritual base. Then I met this man at a local dance in a hotel. We seemed to hit it off, but he was younger than me. I was thirty-six, he was thirty. I wondered about the age difference, but it didn't really seem to matter, somehow. It was a whirlwind romance, and he proposed after the third date. Two weeks later I said 'yes'. We married seven months after meeting. He said, "We should start a family, you know. We should think about a baby, because we're getting on a bit." After we married, it took six months to get pregnant - I was thirty-seven and totally over the moon. My husband was utterly delighted. I had terrible morning sickness, but the pregnancy didn't last for more than six weeks. That hit us hard. So hard that my husband actually had a nervous breakdown. He's always been a sensitive type and had trouble with his nerves. But he recovered and we went on holiday to Ibiza, and I got pregnant again.

'This time, I had my second miscarriage at nine weeks. I had a d. and c. and met a lady who had had seven miscarriages before having one child. The second miscarriage didn't seem so bad as the first, although I was thirty-eight by then. I didn't want to give up trying. I had a job where I had to go round people's houses, assessing them. I worked long, stressful hours. I decided that the next time I got pregnant I would take sick leave and rest.

'It took some time to get pregnant again and when I did, I rested for most of the pregnancy. At the beginning of this pregnancy I noticed a bit of spotting and went straight home from work to bed - and never went back. The doctor sent me to hospital and I stayed there sixteen weeks. It was hard being apart from my husband and the birth was no picnic. I went into labour four weeks early. My waters broke and they took me back into hospital, then put me on a drip to induce labour. It was very painful and I didn't have painkillers. They said the baby was being stressed, so it was a forceps delivery. My son, Andrew, was only 4 lb. and 4 oz. when he was born, so he was in an incubator for three weeks; he was very small.

'But motherhood was wonderful. I took to it like a duck to water and I was just forty. I wanted to breastfeed, but it was impossible because of his premature birth. Anyway, three months later, I was pregnant again. We wanted more children and had left off contraception in the hope it would happen again. We were utterly thrilled, until I started to miscarry yet again. It was quite shocking. I was lying in bed with a baby beside me, my husband at work, and bleeding like mad. When my husband came home I was whisked off to hospital and my mother, who was still with it then, came to look after the baby while I had another d. and c. 'Even so, we decided we would try again and when I was forty-one, I got pregnant again. This pregnancy was largely fine, except that I went into labour at twenty-eight weeks. They put me on drips to stop it and I had to stay in hospital for a couple of months. I felt terrible about leaving Andrew, but he went to his grandparents and they were very good. I broke my heart over leaving him, though. I thought that he'd be aware his mummy was gone and that it would damage him. I was told my premature labours were to do with hormone deficiency, so they gave me injections to sustain the pregnancy. When they took me off the drip they sent me home for the weekend, then I went back in at thirty-seven weeks and they allowed me to go ahead with the birth without induction or anything. It was a perfect birth, with no problem at all. Michael was 6 lb. and 2 oz. and he was born when Andrew was two.

'Andrew was a bit bewildered at first, but soon settled down quite well. My husband works at the university in computing and earns well, so I didn't have to go back to work or worry about money. We were very lucky. I was very happy staying home with the boys, I felt it was my choice. I'd worked for years, after all. Now this was the next phase of my life, albeit in my forties. I thought: "I've been through so much to have these children that I don't want to hand them over to someone else, I want to bring them up myself."

'I went on the coil for a wee while after Michael. Then when he got to eighteen months we started to think about whether we should have another one. We went to see my consultant. I was forty-three by then. He told me all the statistics and that my chances of having something wrong, like Down's or spina bifida, were high. We went home and talked it through and decided to risk it. In three weeks, no time at all, I was pregnant again after coming off the coil. When I went to the hospital the doctor said, "She gets pregnant so easily, it's amazing." We decided not to have any tests. I don't know what I would have done if an amniocentesis had shown a bad result. There was no point in having a test if I wasn't going to abort a baby - which I wasn't. So we risked it.

'The pregnancy went smoothly although I went early into labour yet again. I had injections again and had to go into hospital - Andrew was sent to one grandmother, Michael to the other. It was tough for them, but there was nothing else to do. I was in hospital a while again and the birth was induced. I was three weeks early and it was very painful indeed. All I had was gas and air and I never find that very helpful. Ross was born at 6 lb. 3 oz. and I was nearly forty-four. I thought: "I'm getting the hang of this now." However, I asked the doctor to sterilise me and he did it before I came home. I felt my family was complete. Indeed, the boys have all got on very well. I'm a very patient person, although I'm very firm. My boys are so lovely, and they are very loving, too. Having them was a lovely time of my life and I didn't have any trouble with them at all. My husband got on fine with them, although he didn't have as much to do with them when they were small. Now Andrew is twenty-one, Michael is twenty and Ross is eighteen. Andrew's studying architecture, Michael's in freelance computing and Ross is studying music. Michael and Ross are still based at home, although they do a certain amount for themselves, like washing and cooking. I'm now doing a wee bit of writing, short stories and the like. I've actually just completed writing a novel, a historical romance.

'My relationship with the boys is very close and we love each other to bits. They talk to me about their problems and sometimes it's quite harrowing. When Michael fell out with his girlfriend I spent hours talking to him. Sometimes I'll talk about myself to them, especially to the eldest. The boys are proud of me and my age has never been a problem. I don't look my age. In fact, the age difference between myself and my husband hasn't been a problem, either, and people ask me how much older he is than me. My hair is still auburn, and although I have a few facial lines, I keep fit. I exercise on a bike and go swimming. I keep in shape for my health and wellbeing. I have other women friends who have had children in their forties and it's kept them young as well. They think I'm just a couple of years older than themselves, although it's more like fifteen years. I don't worry about the future, because I can see that my boys are independent and well adjusted. Just as long as they are happy, that's all I care about. I wouldn't have missed having my boys for all the world. I feel very fulfilled, and I couldn't imagine my life without them. I have found the job very tiring, but extremely rewarding. If you can get through it, it is completely worth it. My husband and I are always saying how very, very lucky we are.'

Help and Further Reading

Books

Deciding to have a baby/pregnancy

Cope With Your Biological Clock: How To make the Right Decision About Motherhood, Theresa Francis-Cheung (Hodder, 2001)

First Baby After Thirty... or Forty, Dr Penny Stanway (Orion, 1999)

How to Have a Baby and Stay Sane, Virginia Ironside (Unwin Hyman, 1989)

Not Too Late - Having a Baby After Thirty-five: A Practical and Comprehensive Guide to Pregnancy and Birth, Gill Thorn (Bantam Books, 1998)

Older Mothers: Conception, Pregnancy and Birth After Thirty-five, Julia Berryman, Karen Thorpe and Kate Windridge (Pandora, 1995)

The New Pregnancy and Childbirth, Sheila Kitzinger (Penguin, 1997)

The Baby Challenge: A Handbook on Pregnancy for Women With A Physical Disability, Mukti Jain Campion (Routledge, 1990)

What to Expect When You're Expecting, Arlene Eisenberg, Heidi E. Murkoff and Sandee E. Hathaway (Simon & Schuster, 1996)

Miscarriage

Miscarriage: What Every Woman Needs To Know, Professor Lesley Regan (Bloomsbury, 1997)

Miscarriage: Women's Experiences and Needs, Christine Moulder (Pandora, 1995)

Women's Health

Come Alive: Your Six Point Plan for Lasting Health and Energy, Beth MacEoin (Hodder, 2000)

Feel Fabulous Over Fifty, Gloria Hunniford and Jan de Vries (Hodder, 2000)

Overcoming Addiction: Positive Steps for Breaking Free of Addiction and Building Self-Esteem, Corinne Sweet (Piatkus, 2001)

Women's Bodies, Women's Wisdom: The Complete Guide to Women's Health and Wellbeing, Dr Christine Northrup (Piatkus, 1998)

Abortion

Understanding Abortion, Mary Pipes (The Women's Press, 1986)

Organisations

Action on Pre-Eclampsia (APEC)
Helpline: 01386 761848
https://action-on-pre-eclampsia.org.uk

Barnardo's (for adoption information)
Tel: 0800 0277 280
https://www.barnardos.org.uk/fosteringandadoption

CoramBAAF (British Agencies for Adoption and Fostering)
Tel: 020 7520 0300
https://corambaaf.org.uk/fostering-adoption

British Pregnancy Advisory Service
Head Office Tel: 0345 365 5050
Treatment queries: 03457 30 40 30
https://www.bpas.org

Child Maintenance Service
Tel: 0800 171 2345
https://childmaintenanceservice.direct.gov.uk

COTS (surrogacy information)
Tel: 0333 772 1549
https://www.surrogacy.org.uk

Down's Syndrome Association
Helpline: 0333 1212 300
https://www.downs-syndrome.org.uk

Endometriosis Society UK
Tel: 020 7222 2781
Helpline: 0808 808 2227
https://www.endometriosis-uk.org

Friends of Chernobyl's Children
Tel: 0145 5285 799
https://www.focc.org.uk

Gingerbread
Tel: 0207 428 5400
Helpline: 0808 802 0925
www.gingerbread.org.uk

Fertility Network
Tel: 01424 732 361
Support Line: 0121 323 5025
http://fertilitynetworkuk.org

Maternity Action
Tel: 0207 253 2288
Advice Line: 0808 802 0029
https://www.maternityalliance.org.uk

Miscarriage Association
Helpline: 01924 200799
https://www.miscarriageassociation.org.uk

Family and Childcare Trust (formerly National Family & Parenting Institute)
Tel: 020 7239 7535 https://www.familyandchildcaretrust.org

National Childbirth Trust (NCT)
Support line: 0300 330 0700
https://www.nct.org.uk

NHS 111 (for urgent medical problems, in place of NHS Direct)
Tel: 111
https://111.nhs.uk

ActionAid (sponsor a child)
Tel: 01460 238000
https://www.actionaid.org.uk/sponsor-a-child

Working Families
Tel: 0207 153 1230
Legal advice: 0300 012 0312 https://www.workingfamilies.org.uk

Family Lives (formerly Parentline Plus)
Tel: 0207 553 3080
Helpline: 0808 800 2222 https://www.familylives.org.uk

Recurrent Miscarriage Clinic
(Professor Lesley Regan) Winston Churchill Building, Second Floor, St Mary's Hospital, Praed Street, Paddington, London
W2 1NY
Tel: 020 3312 1117

Stillbirth and Neonatal Death Society (SANDS)
Tel: 0207 436 7940
Helpline: 0808 164 3332
https://www.sands.org.uk

Twins and Multiple Births Association (TAMBA)
Tel: 01252 332 344
https://www.tamba.org.uk

Older Mothers' Website

www.mothers35plus.co.uk
Set up by Lindsey Harris for older mothers - information, noticeboard, etc.